D0354150

Praise for Honesty Sells

"I just wanted to tell you about my success yesterday using your voicemail technique. I was getting frustrated trying to reach this potential client, and I left a message yesterday morning advising her I would call her back at 3 PM, using your techniques from *Honesty Sells*. Sure enough she answered the phone (finally) and I got the business from her."

—*Helen Lightfoot*, HelmsBriscoe

"This material is great! I've applied your ideas and suggestions and it really works!!! Prospecting was my biggest nemesis . . . [and] it isn't anymore. I get weekly appointments, followed by quotations and committed orders."

—*Julia Zenga*

HONESTY
SELLS

HONESTY SELLS

How to Make More Money and Increase Business Profits

STEVEN GAFFNEY

and

COLLEEN FRANCIS

WILEY

JOHN WILEY & SONS, INC.

Published by John Wiley & Sons, Inc., Hoboken, New Jersey.
Published simultaneously in Canada.

For general information on our other products and services or for technical support, please
contact our Customer Care Department within the United States at (800) 762-2974, outside
the United States at (317) 572-3993 or fax (317) 572-4002.

Wiley also publishes its books in a variety of electronic formats. Some content that appears in
print may not be available in electronic books. For more information about Wiley products,
visit our web site at www.wiley.com.

Library of Congress Cataloging-in-Publication Data:

Gaffney, Steven, 1963-
  Honesty sells : how to make more money and increase business
profits / Steven Gaffney, Colleen Francis.
     p. cm.
  Includes bibliographical references and index.
  ISBN 978-0-470-41153-7 (cloth)
  1. Selling—Moral and ethical aspects. 2. Honesty. 3.
Business ethics. I. Francis, Colleen, 1970– II. Title.
  HF5438.25.G34 2009
  174'.4—dc22

                                                    2008700293

Printed in the United States of America

10 9 8 7 6 5 4 3 2 1

Trust is like the air we breathe . . . when it's present, nobody really notices. But when it's absent, everybody notices.
—Warren Buffett

From Colleen

I would like to dedicate this book to my husband, Chris, who is the source of energy and love for everything I do. You inspire me every day. And to my Mom and Dad who always believed that I could do anything I put my mind to . . . including sell!

From Steven

To my Mom and Dad for always loving me even when I was not loveable and Tu-Anh who is the loving angel in my life.

CONTENTS

ACKNOWLEDGMENTS

We are so grateful to so many people who have contributed their stories, wisdom, and coaching to make our work possible and hopefully this book will contribute and make a difference in people's lives. There are many involved in the production of one book and we would like to acknowledge first our clients, participants, family, and friends whose encouragement and stories helped bring this book to life.

To everyone at Wiley, including Matt Holt who believed in our work and ultimately wanted to make this book happen; Jessica Campilango and Dan Ambrosio whose advice, support, and coaching were instrumental in making this book the best it could be. Thank you!

To our Agent Charlotte Gusay, who gave everything she had to make this book happen and make this the best book possible. We are so grateful for your support.

For Casey at Engage who works tirelessly on behalf of our clients and allows me to serve the people and profession I love with ease. Thanks for your belief in and excitement for our business.

To all the staff at Steven Gaffney Company, including my long-time business associate, Christina Taylor, for her endless support and belief in the work I do as well as all that she did to make this work happen.

And a special thanks to all those who helped edit, add to, review, and advise on the draft of this book: Nina Taylor, Patrick Gant, David Elver, and Chris Voice.

INTRODUCTION

Another Book on Sales? Why You Need to Read This Book

There are lots of books on selling. In fact, every year it seems that at least 100 more are published on the topic. So why should you read *Honesty Sells* above all others?

Sure, this book is all about selling. And it's more. It's more than just a how-to guide on selling products or services, though; it explains how you can achieve your maximum potential by unlocking what every top-performing sales professional has perfected to an art—the ability to sell yourself openly and honestly!

Only 10 percent of salespeople in any organization are top performers, defined as those who regularly close at least half of their qualified prospects. At the other end of the spectrum in any given sales force is the bottom 10 percent: underperformers. Underperformers include those who are too new to measure or so bad they are on their way out.

The remaining 80 percent of salespeople fall into a broad category that is best described as mediocre, which applies to salespeople who close about one in three qualified prospects. Few sales professionals would ever choose to be considered mediocre. After all, consider the missed opportunities. While regularly hitting average sales targets, mediocre salespeople are missing out on over two-thirds of potential business that's left unclosed! No one likes to feel as if they've missed an opportunity and—let's face it—now more than ever, no one can afford to lose sales.

What does it take to go from being simply average to becoming a top-ranked sales professional?

That's the core question answered in this book.

Honest communication is at the heart of the solution. One of the key struggles for salespeople everywhere is to communicate openly with clients and prospects. Most complain that it's downright impossible to get their prospects to do this. When was the last time you complained to a manager, a colleague, or a friend that you felt you were not getting the whole truth from a prospect or a client—that they were holding something back?

Those who are in the top 10 percent of the sales profession have mastered the art of open, honest communication with their clients. They've overcome all communication barriers because they understand that every dimension of sales is affected by their ability to engage in meaningful dialogue. Their clients know they can expect integrity and honesty from them in their sales interactions; and that's why they give the same in return.

Here are some questions to consider. Have you ever:

- Found yourself in a situation where a prospect said one thing in a meeting and then did the exact opposite of what they said they would do?
- Lost a sale without knowing why?
- Lost the business because you could never get hold of the prospect again after the proposal was sent or the presentation was completed?
- Had a client leave you for the competition without telling you why or giving you a chance to win them back?

Why do these kinds of situations occur? And just as important—how can you prevent them from happening again and again?

This book has answers—not quick fixes, gimmicky systems, tricks, flimsy techniques. It will not attempt to teach you how to manipulate people to do what you want. Rather, *Honesty Sells* demonstrates how an optimum model of sales behavior—one that is used by the top 10 percent of sales performers everywhere—he can help you build an open, honest, and profitable relationship with your clients.

Important Things You Need to Know

The ideas, strategies, and techniques presented here really work. They are field-tested and will bring you more business faster and easier than ever before. These results are achievable by anyone, regardless of background or personality. The client examples are true. It would be ironic for us to include false examples and made-up stories in a book about honesty, don't you think?

You will learn how to:

- Eliminate communication breakdowns and personality conflicts with even the most difficult clients.
- Ensure your voice mail messages are returned more often.
- Secure more referrals and close more deals faster while keeping clients longer.
- Ensure that clients, prospects, and internal resources do what they say they will do.
- Handle objections quickly and profitably.

Two Final Notes

1. There is an ongoing debate about whether "customer" or "client" is the right term to use in your business. Either is fine. For the purposes of clarity we have chosen to use "client" to define anyone who gives you money in exchange for a product or a service or has the potential to do so. In your own business you may call them customers, friends, family, or clients. All are fine. Just know that we are referring to the same person.

2. We use plenty of examples throughout this book to explain key points. These are based on true accounts, but in some cases names and occupations and some details have been changed to protect the innocent! We need to be honest about the facts of the stories and examples, but as you can imagine not everyone wants their fatal sales mistakes revealed in such a public forum. On the other hand, Colleen and Steven have made so many mistakes, and shared them with clients as examples, they are not afraid or embarrassed by them anymore, so we feel no need to change our own identities!

Top 10 Sales Hall of Shame: When Bad Salespeople Go Even Worse

After more than 15 years in the sales business, we've seen some of the very best this profession has to offer—and more than a few of the worst. The following definitely fall into the latter category. We call them the Top 10 Sales Hall of Shame—a listing of the 10 worst sales practices we've ever had the misfortune to stumble upon, culled from our own personal experience as well as submissions from clients, colleagues, and fellow sales practitioners. The examples below are all true. You may laugh, you may cringe, you may even think, "There is *no way* I would ever do that!" Regardless of your reaction, we encourage you to take note of the lesson in each story. And. before you read any further, we urge you to make sure you haven't got a weak stomach, and please—leave the lights on . . .

They can reach us in our homes. They track us down when we're at the office or on the road. And unless you've spent the last 30 years living on the moon or under a rock, odds are, you've fallen prey to them more than once.

Bad salespeople. Not just bad—beyond bad.

Whether it's the telemarketer who won't take no for an answer, the cold caller who swears she went to school with your dear Uncle Al or the retail salesperson who simply refuses to give you a straight answer, these are the people who give all salespeople—most of whom are decent, honest, hardworking members of the community—a reputation that hovers somewhere between arms dealer and professional heroin merchant.

What's even worse (at least from a sales point of view) is that the vast majority of these misguided, wrongheaded, or just plain dishonest approaches don't work. So while these lowest-of-the-low are out there busily giving all salespeople a bad name, they're also likely just as busy working themselves out of what could have been a promising career.

iPhone, uPhone, We All Phone

From Chris:

> In Canada, a national cell phone provider was recently granted exclusive rights to carry the much-awaited new iPhone.
>
> Not two days after this landmark announcement had played all over the television, radio, and Internet, a representative from one of that provider's biggest competitors called me out of the blue. Apparently, he just wanted to share with me the wonderful news that they would be able to offer me the iPhone too!
>
> Now, my wife and I were as eager as everyone else on the planet to get our hands on these shiny new gadgets. But we also knew beyond a shadow of a doubt that only one company had the iPhone in Canada, and it was definitely not the company with which I was speaking.
>
> As politely as I could, I told the salesperson that we were indeed getting iPhones, but that we would be sticking with Company X, which actually had the right to sell them to us. Undaunted, the salesperson insisted that his Company Y was carrying the iPhone as well and practically demanded that we sign up with them instead.
>
> Still as politely as possible, I reminded him that his firm couldn't possibly offer the iPhone, because (a) its non-GSM network couldn't support it, and (b) it was public knowledge that Company X had an exclusive contract with Apple.
>
> Despite my repeated protestations, he continued to insist that he could supply us with iPhones and demanded that we

switch to his company. After trying without success to make him realize (or admit) the truth, I finally just hung up.

Needless to say, we are now very happy with our new iPhones and Company X. As for Company Y—let's just say, we haven't exactly been seeing "i" to "i."

It's the Factory's Fault!

From Amanda:

When it came time to buy our current car, I tried my best to do everything the experts say we all should.

I did my research. I identified which manufacturer, make, and model I was interested in. I even picked out a color and made a list of all the options I wanted. In short, everything was going perfectly according to plan.

That is, until I took the test drive.

To make sure I was going to get the best deal, I decided to test drive my chosen vehicle at three different dealerships in three cities. The first two went just fine. I drove the car (with standard transmission, my preferred choice). The salespeople were both helpful and professional. I got my price quotes from them, and went on to the last dealer on my list.

When I arrived at the third dealer, I asked if I could take the car I wanted for a drive—same make, same transmission, same everything. Only this time, the salesperson told me that they didn't have a standard version of the car, and asked if I'd like to try an automatic instead.

I thanked him, said I preferred standard and started to walk away. But before I could leave, he begged me to wait for a moment while he checked with his manager.

When he came back, he told me that I wouldn't have any luck finding the car I wanted with any transmission other than automatic. Why? Because, he told me with an apologetic smile, the factory had decided not to make any this year.

I guess the standard models at the other two dealerships must've been the product of some kind of automotive Immaculate Conception.

A Little Sizzle with Your Steak?

From Susan:

I like the warm summer months as much as the next gal. Maybe more. But even for me, heat has its limits.

One particular August, it had been over 100 degrees—and humid—without letup for about a week. Our grass was turning brown. Our dog wouldn't go outside. And my husband and I were trying to figure out how to hook up our lemonade supply intravenously.

On the hottest day of that hottest week, I got a call from a salesperson asking if I had received the free sample of meat his company had sent me in the mail.

Meat. Sent by mail. In 100-plus degree weather.

Even in my heat-addled state of mind, it was pretty obvious that he hadn't sent me any samples and was only calling to get me to request information about his company's products.

It was almost enough to make me become a vegetarian.

Ms. President, I Presume?

From Cheryl:

One day while I was working on a sales presentation, I got a call at the office from a company sales rep trying to sell me an updated web site. I asked the sales rep how he had gotten my name and number, and he told me that he had spoken personally with the president of the association I belonged to, and *he* had given the company permission to call all the members to see if they wanted to upgrade.

Sounds convincing, right? There was just one problem: I happened to have the honor of serving as president of the association that year, and I had never even heard of this company, let alone given them permission to contact our membership.

My guess is, they had simply gotten our member profiles off of the association web site, and were using this lie to try to sell us their service. A shame that, while they were online, they hadn't taken the time to note down the president's name—or gender!

The Blind Leading . . . Period

From Brent:

One of my first jobs in sales was working as a rep for a large copier company. I can still remember the day I made my first sale of a brand new copier to the Institute for the Blind.

It wasn't a top-of-the-line machine, but it was a solid sale, and I couldn't have been happier. I treated myself to a celebratory cup of coffee (extra cream and sugar) and went to tell my manager the good news.

The party didn't last long.

When I told him the particulars of the sale, he ordered me to send the client a used copier instead of a new one because, and I quote: "they won't be able to tell the difference."

I quit the next week. As for my manager, I can only hope he got everything he deserved. Like, say, a transfer to the branch office in Siberia.

Made in China

From Tim:

Several years ago, the company I was working for at the time decided to save a little money by phasing out a successful product line that had been made in Canada for many years and substituting it with one that came from China.

That's all well and good. The only problem was, they didn't advise their clients—or their sales team.

Four months later, we were all called together for a North American sales meeting and asked if there had been any quality issues with the product line. None of us had received any specific client complaints, so they told us about the switch they had made, and congratulated themselves heartily on their success.

A few months later, one of my biggest accounts called to ask me about a change they had noticed in the quality of the product they'd been ordering from us for years. They asked me if anything had recently changed, and I dutifully told them that we now had a partner in China making the product to our specifications, and we had been shipping this instead.

For the next 15 minutes, the client proceeded to tear a huge strip off me for not advising him of the change. He was upset with my company for making the change in the first place, but even more furious with *me* for not advising him of the change when I first heard about it.

I learned a valuable lesson that day. My company could have launched the made-in-China product as an economy line at a lower price and still made a respectable profit.

Instead, by keeping the change a secret from both its employees and its clients, the company cost itself—and me!— one of our oldest and most loyal clients.

Get It in Writing

From Casey:

I was negotiating a few years back with a major hotel chain for a large event that we were hosting at one of its finer properties. Because of the importance of the event, I made sure to lay out every detail of what we needed at every step of the negotiations.

The hotel's RFP response clearly stated that there would be no food and beverage minimum. But in its second written response a short while later, the hotel demanded a minimum food and beverage order of no less than $50,000.

When I called to confirm the numbers, they told me that the $50,000 minimum was in fact for every two days of the event, making the total tally that much higher.

I spoke with my partner, and while neither of us was happy with the magically changing numbers, we agreed to go ahead as planned. The hotel sent over the final contract to be signed, and sure enough, it laid out our minimum food and beverage order of $50,000—*per day.*

They had missed deadline after deadline in sending us the information, and when the contract finally did arrive, none of the clauses we had agreed to by e-mail were included in the paperwork.

It was too late for us to do anything at the time but swallow our anger, strain our budget, and proceed with the event. But you can bet that was the last time either my partner or I used the services of that particular hotel chain.

Just Sign Right Here . . .

From Christopher:

I was approached at home one day by a door-to-door salesperson selling an energy contract. His rates sounded reasonable, so I asked him if he could give me a firm quote based on our home and general energy usage.

He told me that he would be more than happy to give me a quote, but to get it, I would have to sign some paperwork authorizing him to look into how much we could save by moving to his service.

I noticed that the paperwork he gave me to sign had the word "contract" written in big, bold letters across the top of it. I asked him point blank if what I was signing was a contract, and he immediately assured me that it was not.

I wanted to make absolutely certain that what I was signing was just an authorization to get a quote, so I asked him again in a different way along the lines of: "So by signing this, I will in no way be locked into any kind of agreement to buy energy from you at a specified price over a set period of time. You are *not* locking me into *anything*. Correct?"

Once again, he assured me that this was not a contract, and I would not be locked into anything in any way.

In order to process my quote, we had to call his head office to confirm a few details. In the course of our conversation, I asked the head office agent if the paper I was signing was a contract. She replied that yes, it certainly was, and by signing it, I would be locking myself in for three years at a fixed rate.

I couldn't believe the blatant lie the door-to-door sales rep had told me. After thanking the head office agent, I hung up and happily kicked him out the door. Thank goodness not everyone in his organization was as deceitful as him.

Parlez-Vous Français?

From Eliot:

One of my responsibilities with a former employer was to hire a new sales rep for a bilingual position (French/English) to serve our overseas clients.

I received many resumes written in both languages. Several of them included a note explaining that the potential candidate spoke a third language as well—usually Spanish or German.

The resume of one particularly promising candidate indicated that she was proficient in English, French, and Spanish. So halfway through the interview, I suddenly switched to French. I asked her a question that would be simple for anyone with even a rudimentary understanding of the language to answer, but it was obvious from the look on her face that she hadn't a clue what I was saying.

Sensing that she might not have been completely honest with me, I switched to Spanish. She was equally lost. To give her one last chance to redeem herself (and allow myself to blow off a little steam after having been misled for the better part of the morning), I asked her, in Spanish, if she was a liar.

When my question was once more met with a deer-in-the-headlights look and stunned silence, I switched back to English, gave her back her resume and asked her to leave.

Funny—this time she seemed to get the message fast enough.

It'll Be Here Next Week—Honest!

From Cindy:

During the sales process with a large, government-owned central bank, the client asked if we could support an expensive database they already had in house. We told them that our product couldn't currently support their database, but it would be able to in the next release, which was expected to be available within the next few months.

Based on the promise that we would be able to meet their specs soon, they bought our product, and just worked around the limitations until the next release came through.

Five years and a constant flow of compatibility problems later, the COO of our company was visiting the client on-site one day when he was asked when the support for their database would be ready.

He assured them that it would be part of the next release. The client's answer was to pull out a sheaf of five letters, signed by our company's top executives over each of the past five years, all claiming that the modification was coming "in the next release."

Since we had been releasing new versions of the software each year, it was clear that we had simply chosen to ignore their request and then lied to them about it. Not just the salespeople, either, but the technology, marketing, sales and product management executives as well—all in writing.

Needless to say, we were kicked out and replaced by a company willing to be honest about its capabilities from the start. In all my years in sales, I've never seen a more just or well-deserved dismissal.

Honesty—The Best Policy for Closing Sales and Growing the Business

H onesty sells. It sounds almost like a joke, doesn't it? The words honesty and sales are two words that aren't usually paired. *We* think they are made for each other. Together they make the most powerful and effective strategy for long-term sales success.

Just how do honesty and sales work together? That's what we're here to show you: specific strategies for honest communication that will make a positive impact on your ability to gain new clients and earn repeat sales. Most people may not connect honesty and sales, and when you do, you'll revolutionize your ability to gain the confidence of your clients and enjoy sales success.

What Is Honest Communication?

Honesty. It sounds like a simple word, and Webster's definition of the term is just that. "Honesty: a fairness and straightforwardness of conduct; adherence to the facts." We define honest communication as saying what needs to be said—including all the pertinent facts.

Honesty is not about sharing every single thought and opinion. We are advocating honesty, not brutality. If you thought one of your clients was not too bright, we certainly wouldn't suggest you share that opinion in the guise of "honest communication." Not at all. The key to honest communication is saying what needs to be said in a situation and not withholding what others need to know.

Has anyone ever withheld information from you? Not letting you know that things weren't going as expected? When you found out the truth, how did you feel? If you are like most people, you felt lied to.

All of us withhold information, the question is what are we withholding? After all, we all have more thoughts in our heads than we can possibly share with our mouths. Because we can't share everything, we are always self-selecting what should be said. Said differently, we all withhold.

Withholding information can be a slippery slope. For instance, salespeople are often faced with a situation in which their company is behind on delivery. What if you found yourself in that situation? You might think that there's no need to tell the client. Why worry them? That line of thinking seems legitimate. But at what point should you break your silence and tell the client? How late is too late to tell the truth? The trouble with withholding such information is that when clients find out that things are behind schedule and you weren't upfront about it, they feel lied to and will begin micromanaging you and the sales process to control the outcome. This can be the beginning of the end.

When a client feels he's been lied to, it leads to distrust and micromanaging. And when it comes time to look at additional purchases, that client most often will not repurchase from you. Our own studies show that when trust is not present, there is only a 2 percent chance that a client will reorder from an existing supplier. As well, such clients certainly won't recommend you to others. Honest communication has the opposite effect. It builds trust, ensures sales, additional sales, and referrals. Let's look at the power of honesty and its power to turn around a bad situation and build relationships.

Honesty Builds and Maintains Credibility

Several years ago when Zemira Jones was general sales manager of WMAL radio in Washington, D.C., he received a call from one of his salespeople, Jane. Jane was distressed. She had received a phone call from a client, Kristine, one of the top media buyers in New York City. Kristine requested that Jane send her a short memo confirming that the station had given away her client's in-store coupons over the past few weekends as part of an on-air contest. Jane called the weekend on-air personality to confirm the coupons had been given away. They had not.

The issue was bigger than it appeared because of a pending order from this media buyer for a new campaign. That business was worth hundreds of thousands of dollars to the radio station. A big sale. Jane knew Zemira's strong feelings about complete honesty and transparency at all levels at the station, but she wanted permission to lie under these circumstances. She thought the stakes were high enough to warrant it. Jane was worried that not only would the station suffer a financial loss, but it could suffer a loss of reputation as well.

Despite the many concerns, Zemira was unequivocal in his answer. He said they should tell the truth—that they must always tell the truth. Zemira told her that the station would take full responsibility for its inaction. He said Jane should tell the client the truth and how the situation would be addressed.

Faced with a Similar Situation, What Might You Do?

Like Zemira, many of us believe that honesty is the best policy. The trouble is that we often believe it in theory rather than practice. Like Jane, when we feel backed into a corner, we think lying or withholding the truth is the better policy. When we interviewed Zemira about this situation, he explained that he believes honesty is a key business strategy that impacts the bottom line. We couldn't agree more.

In this particular situation, when the salesperson told the client the truth, the client was pleasantly surprised. The buyer was so impressed that the salesperson had told the truth when it would have been so easy to lie (no documentation other than the memo was required) that her image of the radio station soared. Its reputation and credibility were reinforced, and it won the pending business. Telling the truth not only resolved the situation, it helped to solidify the relationship. After this incident, the station received even more business from this big media buyer.

Are you surprised? We aren't. We know from our own experience in sales and through our work as consultants that honest communication is the number one long-term strategy for sales and business growth. Honesty takes us where we want to go—from closing the sale to gaining repeat business.

Lesson 1: The truth helps to bond relationships and build trust—especially when there are problems. People don't always like what they hear when you tell the truth but they respect your integrity and your courage. And that respect helps to build the most fundamental building block of all relationships: trust.

Lesson 2: Trust builds business. People say they do business with people they like. We have found that is not 100 percent accurate. The more accurate statement is that people do business with people who they like *and* trust. Like is important because it leads to trust. But it is the trust that ultimately wins the sale. It is no accident that in WMAL's case likeability and trust helped win future business.

Lesson 3: Telling the truth to clients influences the organization internally. When Zemira reinforced the fact that his policy was always to tell the truth, Jane knew that she could trust him to be honest with her. So not only is honesty a great sales strategy (as we'll be discussing throughout this book), it is also a key leadership strategy within an organization, resulting in greater trust and loyalty between managers and staff.

As an interesting side note, Zemira went on to become president and general manager at ABC Radio-Chicago and later held the position of vice president of operations for Radio One Inc., the seventh largest radio company in the country. We would agree with Zemira about that childhood maxim, honesty really is the best policy.

Honesty. Loyalty. Trust. These are powerful concepts we all believe in theory and can easily forget in practice. Sometimes when push comes to shove, people toss the value of honesty aside, because in a crunch it's easy to think that telling the truth is not the best idea after all. We're afraid that if we share the whole truth, we may lose the sale. In fact, what we learn from examples like Zemira's is that telling the truth can ultimately gain the client's confidence, make sales, and win future business.

Withholding the truth is a short-term strategy. The news is rife with reminders of this reality: People, your clients always find out the truth in the end. These reminders come from all walks of life—business, sports, and even publishing. Look at Enron, WorldCom, Martha Stewart, Marion Jones, Rafael Palmeiro, and James Frey. In each case, the truth came out. Sometimes it took a while, but it happened. You can probably think of your own cast of characters famous for lying and withholding. Thanks to the Internet it doesn't take as long as it used to for the world to learn about our mistakes. Today, the potential damage from lying is greater than in the past.

Once trust has been lost, it is difficult to reestablish it, and business and potential business can be lost forever.

Summing Up

Fortunately, there's no need to toss honesty aside and resort to withholding information to win a sale while we risk our reputation. Like Zemira we can communicate with openness and honesty, even admitting a past mistake, and close the sale while simultaneously improving our reputation and relationship. That's the value and power of honest communication in sales and in all of life—its ability to transcend difficulty and build relationships. Once we begin to act on this truth, we can apply the strategy of honest communication to our business and sales opportunities and experience long-term gain. Profitably.

The Startling Truth about Why Honesty Sells

I t seems everyone has had an experience with a less-than-honest salesperson. We'll bet you've heard some stories yourself. Perhaps you experienced some similar or worse than those listed in the Sales Hall of Shame in Chapter 1. We're not saying that all salespeople are dishonest. Not at all. But like it or not, that reputation precedes all of us who sell.

Clients may not believe this, but most salespeople have their own stories to tell. We bet you do, too. Have you ever felt like a client or a prospect wasn't being totally honest with you? Well, the bad news is that possibly they were not. According to James Patterson and Peter Kim, authors of *The Day America Told the Truth: What People Really Believe About Everything That Really Matters*, 91 percent of people admit to lying regularly to family, friends, and associates—91 percent! It's no wonder buyers and sellers have had a history of contemptuous behavior.

It's an unsettling statistic and yet it's an all-too-common complaint made by clients about salespeople—and vice versa. To borrow an adage, in sales—like war—the truth often tends to be the first casualty. Let's consider what compels people—both salespersons and clients—to lie.

Why Salespeople Lie to Clients

Ask almost anyone to describe a salesperson and you won't hear the most flattering terms. Huckster, snake-oil peddler, fast-talking con artist, swindler, liar. How did we ever get such a fine reputation? It is unfortunate. Those of us who sell today do so in an environment created by a few unscrupulous salespeople in it for the short term and the short-term buck. These unprofessional hucksters are not interested in creating long-term profitable relationships with their clients.

The reality is there are many reasons why salespeople lie to their clients. Here are three major ones:

1. *They don't know their product.* Some salespeople lie because they are insecure or unsure about the products they are selling. In short, sometimes they are too embarrassed to say, "I don't know." Have you ever met someone who doesn't know his stuff? Frustrating, isn't it? Wouldn't you prefer the person just admit it? If you're anything like us, then you'd at least like to hear the salesperson say, "I don't know, but I'll get the information you're requesting and get back to you."

2. *They are too empathetic and they don't like conflict.* Some salespeople lie because they are insecure about themselves and their relationship with the prospect. For some salespeople, the driving factor is "I just want the client to like me!" In the process of trying to build a friend first and a client second, they lie, telling the client what he wants to hear. Salespeople who lie out of insecurity will work to preserve the relationship at all costs and are often notorious for overpromising and underdelivering. Salespeople in this category promise to send out a client's proposal by Thursday—only to ship it out Monday of the following week.

3. *They are only focused on the money.* Some salespeople see lying as the only way to make a quick buck. They are focused on greed instead of helping clients. Salespeople

who lie for this reason do it because they want the prospect to move too quickly so that they can make a quick sale, pocket the commission, and move on to the next prospect. In our opinion, these are not so much salespeople as "con-people." They use tricks and techniques that are designed to railroad a client into making a decision. Now there's nothing wrong with making money, but there is a problem with this approach. The problem doesn't just affect the clients; in the end these lies will catch up to the salespeople, too.

The fact is that salespeople who lie will eventually be found out and lose all credibility in the eyes of a potential client. Ironically, they then lose their ability to close the fastest and most profitable business there is—the repeat sale—because it is virtually impossible to sell more to a client who does not trust you. In fact, a study of decision makers by Bill Brooks and Tom Travasono published in *You're Working Too Hard to Make the Sale* showed that in 98 percent of the cases where clients do not trust their salesperson, they will shop around when they need to reorder!

Honesty Will Hurt Sales

It's true. You may know a very successful salesperson who lies. We do not deny that possibility. Some people believe that lying is effective in making short-term sales. Lying is not a profitable long-term strategy. The current subprime housing and mortgage debacle in the United States is a great case in point. Many unscrupulous lenders duped unsuspecting clients into terrible mortgage deals. If those lenders were still in business, do you think any of those clients would ever come back for repeat business? No way! Lying produced a lot of "success" in the short term, but the long-term success will be zero.

This leads to an important point. As you read this book, you may think of a situation in which you were honest and you lost the business or didn't get the sale. Unfortunately, when things like that happen, we tend to get spooked. Instead, remember that nothing works 100 percent of the time. Don't toss out the standard because of a setback. Honesty builds trust; integrity in your communication will pay off. And remember the top 10 percent of salespeople practice honesty as the best long-term strategy to build business and profits.

It is honesty with ourselves and with our potential and actual clients that establishes and maintains our credibility. Honesty means not lying to your prospects or clients either by what you say or by what you choose not to say. Dishonesty and withholding information is never a good strategy. It shouldn't be rationalized and it does affect sales outcomes.

Let's look at the issue of dishonesty from a client's perspective. Consider Anna's experience, described here: (which could also make the Hall of Shame as item 11!)

> My husband and I were shopping for a new car. We found one we liked and the sales rep was friendly, helpful, and treated us with respect . . . until after the test drive, when he leaned over the hood of the car, looked me straight in the eye, and said: "You know, that's a really popular car you're looking at. I sold 50 of them last year. This steel-gray one you like is hot. I can guarantee that unless you put a deposit on this last gray one today, this car won't be here on Monday."
>
> I normally would have either laughed or just walked away, but I was so shocked at his approach that I couldn't resist firing back:
>
> Me: Are you using the "impending-doom close" on me?
> Salesman (flustered): Excuse me?

Me: You know the impending-doom close. It's an old closing tactic where you tell me that if I don't take action today, there's a risk that the opportunity won't be available tomorrow. Are you actually trying to tell me that the factory is never going to make another gray car again?

Needless to say, he lost the sale. And we bought the car a month later from another dealer who had plenty of steel-gray cars on his lot.

Would you have bought that car, knowing the salesperson was deliberately misleading you? Not likely.

Why Clients Lie to Salespeople

Why do so many clients and prospective clients have so much trouble telling the truth when dealing with salespeople? One of the most common reasons is that they have been lied to in the past by a salesperson. Let's face it, the sales profession has a bad reputation and is considered by some to be among the least-respected occupations. Given this, it's little wonder that clients might be tempted to be selective with the truth! They'll lie to avoid an annoying sales pitch. They'll lie to protect themselves against the persistent phone calls and e-mail follow-ups and to avoid being pressured into making a decision. They'll lie to protect their reputations, their budgets, their time, and their jobs. They'll lie because they can— because they assume all salespeople are liars and they want to make a preemptive strike.

Think about how salespeople are portrayed in popular culture. Movies such as *Tin Men, Planes, Trains and Automobiles, Tommy Boy,* and *Glengarry Glen Ross* don't paint a flattering portrait of this profession. That's a pretty swift current that our profession has to row against. But it's not an impossible challenge. Gaining the trust of your clients and potential clients just takes a little extra effort and forethought, as well as a complete dedication to honesty in how you conduct your business.

What You Can Do

The fact is that dishonesty breeds dishonesty and honesty breeds honesty. This is good news, because it means the ball is in your court. As a salesperson, you truly can help turn the tide with your potential clients and begin to breed more honesty.

Suppose you can sense that your client is withholding information. You can just feel it. Perhaps he's telling you that there's no allocated budget for a purchase. But you know there's almost always some budget. In such a case, you might say, *"Thanks for letting me know. I'm not trying to burn your whole budget. What I want to do is give you the best possible solution within the investment that makes sense. Are you saying there is no budget for any purchase, at any price or just no budget for purchase of the $100,000 project we proposed?"* A direct and honest question expressed without frustration can often provoke prospects to reveal their budgetary constraints.

Honesty must be a two-way street. If it's not, sales and client service will suffer. If a potential client doesn't clearly tell you what they're looking for, it's hard to satisfy the demand. Haven't you ever thought, *I wish they would have told me what they were really looking for*, or *I wish they had just told me their real budget so I didn't waste all this time?* Most of us have. You can't sell if you don't have all the information. This is why two-way, honest, open communication is so necessary.

For example, an IT consult needs to respond to an Request for Proposal (RFP). The more the consulting firm knows about the potential client's needs, the more persuasive its proposal will be. Getting the right information from the client about their needs and budget is essential to customizing a proposal and getting the business.

As salespeople looking to increase sales we need to communicate with honesty and openness, and we need to help others communicate with us in that way. Not only is honest communication the key to long-term sales success, it's crucial in today's work world.

Why Honesty Matters Now More Than Ever

This discussion about lies and honesty is critical today. It used to be that the average unsatisfied client would tell a handful of people about a bad experience. The Internet has changed the game. Now, that same unsatisfied client can share his experiences with millions of people.

Furthermore, Yahoo! estimates that only 56 percent of people trust the information on a corporate web site (Saga Research estimates the numbers are as low as 4 percent), but 87 percent of people trust user testimonials and comments. Given that a full 78 percent of your clients do online research for all products (online and off-line sales), what your clients say about you online will affect your ability to sell. Let's look at a revealing example.

Mary, a software sales rep, was planning her wedding at a beautiful and exclusive European hotel. She booked the entire hotel and all the rooms for her parties and her guests. She was told her guests would have exclusive use of the property. In fact, it was written in her contract.

The hotel sales rep subsequently received a call from the manager of a very famous rock band requesting rooms at the hotel. While they didn't need very many rooms, they did have strict requirements for privacy, security, and all adjacent rooms to be vacant. Desperate to please the rock band, the hotel rep lied and said the hotel was available. She closed off part of the hotel and moved the wedding guests to a different hotel. She did not tell the bridal party and, in fact, told the guests to play along with the lie, asking them not to tell the bridal party.

During the reception the bride's mother found out that more than half the guests had been moved. The hotel managers and reps tried to cover it up, but they had no excuse because of the contract they had signed. The hotel was forced to return money to the wedding party, causing it to lose money that weekend despite the rock stars' fees. But the worst news for the hotel is yet to come. The bride's mother not only told her friends but posted the story on Trip Advisor and other Web-based travel review sites. These sites are frequented by tens of millions of potential travelers.

Given that one unhappy client can go online and tell millions, we're certain you'll agree that lying and withholding information are not worth the risk. Not only does dishonest communication cause you to miss out on repeat business, it can easily ruin your reputation. This is why honesty and sales are no laughing matter.

The Problems with Popular Strategies

Successful salespeople use a range of styles and techniques, and they all share one thing in common: They know that honest communication is the secret to increasing sales effectiveness in the long run. By focusing their efforts on creating a positive client experience based on openness and trust, these professionals sell more, get more referrals, and experience less stress. More than that, it's the easiest sales strategy out there because it's not manipulative.

The trouble with a lot of sales strategies is their insincerity. Such strategies only work if the other person doesn't know what you are doing. If the client realizes you're using a manipulative strategy on them, watch out! It could easily damage your relationship and undermine the potential business.

Have you ever taken a seminar that encourages you to label or categorize people? In this type of training people take a test and categorize people into certain quadrants or groupings. Then they figure out how each group of people likes to be talked to. The theory sounds good. In reality it can be hard to implement.

The truth is that people are not that easy to figure out. Psychologists make a lifetime study of human behavior. And do they ever get it wrong? Sure. How are we ever going to get it right after a training course that lasts a day, two days, or even a month? You're right. It's unlikely, because people are not that simple.

If we try to categorize and analyze our clients, we could be dead wrong. Do all your male clients act alike? Do all managers appear to think the same way? Do all your baby boomer clients make decisions the same way? Of course not. If we judge people by their titles or a characteristic and talk to them accordingly, we most likely won't get the results we're looking for. Besides, who has time for all that personality profiling and categorizing when there are sales to close? A two-way, open, honest conversation with all clients will enable us to discover what our buyers really want and need.

These courses and seminars are not all bad. They can be helpful if they cause us to think more deeply about how to meet individual needs and how to best communicate with others. But we have seen people try to analyze others after these sessions. It's far more effective to realize that all people are different and motivated by different things.

Rather than walking into a meeting and giving the same canned presentation geared toward a stereotyped personality, characteristic, or demographic, wouldn't it be better to engage the clients in some candid conversations? Then the presentation can be adjusted as appropriate to fit the clients' needs and desires. This approach will always be more effective (and profitable) than a sales presentation based on some initial assessment and categorization.

Another popular sales strategy is mirroring. It's a common rapport-building strategy. The idea is to mirror someone's behavior, tone, and tempo of speech in an effort to bond with them. The theory is sound; people like people who are like themselves.

The problem is that if someone catches us doing the monkey-see, monkey-do routine, not only does the strategy become ineffective, it can cause the entire relationship to unravel! When someone is fake, we disconnect. To compound matters, we will then begin to look for more evidence that proves we cannot trust that individual and it sets off a whole downward spiral.

The great thing about honesty is that you're just being yourself. Think about it. People bond most easily with people who they can trust. Honesty and sincerity—or the lack thereof—comes through loud and clear.

The more we act like ourselves, the more likely we are to connect with our clients, establish rapport, and eventually make that sale. It's a lot easier to remember to be yourself than to mirror each of your clients. Phew! That's hard work, and we like to leave the acting up to the paid professional actors.

Summing Up

We advocate honest communication because it's the easiest and most profitable sales strategy available. When communication is honest, everyone says what needs to be said, which eliminates all the figuring out, analyzing, and categorizing—as well as the chance of getting things wrong.

Honest dialogue will provide you with lasting success and measurable results in your work. Applying the advice and insight in this book—based on our experience both as consultants and as sales professionals who have been there—will make a difference. It will help you build your confidence and teach you the steps to take to be prepared for challenges that you will encounter in your sales career.

In short, with the right attitude and a modest investment of your time, this book can help you build lasting solutions, keeping you on the road to professional success. You might be asking yourself: So how do we get there?

In the chapters that follow we'll provide tips and techniques that will help you transform the way you communicate with everyone you encounter on the way to making a sale and keeping the client. Clients, prospects, vendors, suppliers, managers, and colleagues all need to be communicated with honestly in order for you to have the most profitable sales career. We'll explore the way to create two-way, honest, open relationships—the best overall strategy for long-term sales growth. All that's required is a willingness to learn a new and more effective way of doing business with people. It's that simple. The first step? Being honest with yourself.

Being Honest with Yourself

L ying to yourself is another lie to avoid. It is perhaps one of the worst lies we can tell. First, when we lie to ourselves it affects our attitude and our ability to communicate with others. Second, acting like ourselves is more powerful than trying to act like someone else. That's why honesty is more effective than mirroring personality profiling or other strategies that seek to forge a false bond with clients.

To achieve your maximum potential, you must first be honest with yourself. Consider Steven's and Colleen's experience early in their sales careers.

Steven:

My first major job out of college was selling photocopiers; later I was in sales for the Carnation Food Company. To be quite blunt, I wasn't good—in either position. I was actually worse than not good. I was horrible. For the most part, it wasn't until I got involved in the seminar business that I really could sell. Why? Because I believed in it. I saw how these seminars produced results and changed lives. That belief affected my attitude, which in turn affected my potential clients, turning them into actual clients.

Lesson learned. First, you have to be honest with yourself, because honesty and sincerity come through loud and clear.

Colleen:

When I first started in sales I was a complete failure. Need proof? Well, for the first 12 months of my sales career, I sold nothing. Zip. Zilch. Zippo. And to make things worse, not only was I not earning any commissions, I was digging a deep hole of debt. You see, I was paid a draw against earnings of

$2,000 per month whether I sold anything or not. So after selling *nothing* for the first six months, I was left owing the company $12,000. And this was in addition to my car payments, mortgage, and other bills mounting at home.

To help my performance I was given a mentor. Fred. And I was pushed out of the office to figure out what Fred was doing right. This was the start of my mastering a second success secret: behavioral congruence. I quickly learned that I needed to be honest with myself. I needed to believe in what I was selling and truly care about my clients in order to be successful. What was working for Fred could work for me, too, if I applied the ideas with my own style and personality. Quickly, Fred taught me three things about sales that have been the drivers of my success ever since. The key? Be nice by being honest and sales will follow.

The top 10 percent of salespeople know how to steer clear of dangerous assumptions and lies that the mediocre tell themselves in business. That's why in this chapter we've itemized the most lethal assumptions and lies we've witnessed salespeople telling themselves. Some items on the list may seem obvious to you. And that makes them worse. We estimate that a full 80 percent of salespeople tell themselves these lies every day!

Just as important, we've also included advice on what you can do to either avoid committing any of these sins . . . or repent in a hurry.

Assuming That Clients Will Think You Are Being Honest with Them

Even if you have a mantel full of awards at home that say, "The Most Honest Salesperson Ever," you have to constantly prove your honesty and trustworthiness to people you meet.

Sadly, it is a human characteristic that people tend to remember and talk more often about the negative experiences they've had than they do about the positive ones. Consider a bad experience you might have had in the past with a dishonest salesperson. Maybe it was the last time you bought a new car, TV, or even a pair of shoes. That experience, if left unchecked, could influence how you perceive everyone who sells cars, TVs, or shoes—no matter how unfair that kind of judgment would be. As a sales professional, the onus is on you to demonstrate through words and actions that you're the real deal on honesty.

Treating Prospecting as Something You'll Outgrow Eventually

After hitting their targets again and again, some find it tempting to start looking at prospecting as something they don't need to do anymore. Incredibly, sales trainers often hear stories about seasoned salespeople who say *they're too experienced to prospect* . . . or that *cold calling is beneath them.* That's crazy! Prospecting is the lifeblood of a successful sales strategy. It's how you constantly cultivate new business opportunities and grow your client base. Without including this as a fundamental component of your regular business habits, you could be putting your career at serious risk. Everyone needs to prospect . . . no matter how successful they are. To be effective at prospecting, you need to have more than a system for attracting qualified buyers. You also need a sales funnel that's three times larger than what you need in sales. Stuck for ideas on where to find prospects? Check out Exhibit 4.1 for 16 ideas that will keep your funnel full all year long.

Exhibit 4.1   16 Tips to Ensure Your Funnel Is Full

If you find prospecting always somehow slips to the bottom of your "to do" list, here are 16 tips to help you ensure that your sales funnel is consistently full of leads. Note: This is by no means a complete list. It's just a start, to get you thinking and taking action. If you have other ideas please visit www.honestysells.com/blog and post them to the site for us top sales professionals to use and share.

1. Call your existing clients to do an annual review. Look for new opportunities while you are conducting the interview.

2. Conduct a reactivation campaign for previous or lost clients.

3. Set a goal for the number of networking events you will attend each month and the number of new people you'd like to meet at each event. Collect cards, send thank-you notes, and set up meetings.

4. Follow up on trade show leads. Recently we spoke with a trade show organizer who shared with us a shocking statistic—companies report that over 80 percent of all trade show leads are never followed up on.

5. Reward yourself for closing new business. What gets rewarded gets repeated!

6. Purchase targeted opt-in e-mail or direct mail lists in your target area. Plan a marketing campaign.

7. Ask your current clients for referrals. Ask your neighbors for referrals. Ask your family and friends for referrals.

8. Drive around your territory to see who is new, moved, or expanded.

9. Check out online directories for associations in your territory. Build personal relationships with associations and offer to write for their publications.

10. Make a habit of having lunch, coffee, or breakfast with at least one new person each week. Invite people who don't know each other but should and make connections.

11. Write articles for relevant online or print publications your prospects might read.

12. Volunteer to speak at trade shows and conferences. Better yet, ask a client to come along and present a case study of how your product is helping them.

13. Be excellent at what you do! Get a reputation for being world class.

14. Join the trade associations or organizations your clients and prospects belong to.

15. Send monthly mailings to prospects and clients complete with relevant items of interest—not your marketing brochure.

16. Have a holiday campaign, sale, or party. Attract people to your business by celebrating a usual or unusual holiday and make it relevant to the product you are selling.

Thinking That a Great Product Will Sell Itself or That the Competition Is Nonexistent

One of the worst lies that salespeople can tell themselves is this: *People need what I'm selling and they have to buy it from me.* Truthfully, even if your product is something that people really need—for instance, cars, houses, clothing, insurance, or oil—nobody really needs *you*. Prospects have been successful in the past without you, and they will find someone else to do business with if you're gone. In addition, when money is tight and companies are watching their profits (which is always) your competition can be anyone or anything that causes your buyer to be distracted. Here's how you can avoid this deadly sin. Offer your prospects and clients a *great relationship*—one that can help make it easier for them to do business. That's what will keep those clients coming back again and again.

Believing in the Adage "Nothing Personal . . . It's Just Business"

Big mistake. Successful sales professionals will tell you that in business, *everything* is personal and further we believe that if you are serious about your career you should take it personally! People buy from people they like and trust. And that's personal! It's true. In essence, when a client chooses one salesperson over another, what they're really saying is that—other things being equal—they like one better than the other. Great sales records are built on likeability and trust. Likeability is personal. Establishing and maintaining great personal rapport is how you build trust between yourself and your clients.

Relying on a "Low-Hanging Fruit" Strategy to Hit Your Targets

Beware this common trap that ensnares many salespeople. Encouraged by successive quarters of chart-topping sales, it can be very tempting to hit the cruise control button, sit back, and rely on an existing client list to maintain sales. In fact, the most dangerous period a company faces is the one right after a record-breaking quarter. It is a mistake to assume that the market will always be like a bumper crop in which your job is to simply keep picking the low-hanging fruit. In fact, because all markets go up and down—you have to keep your sales machinery in top working order at all times.

Treating Any Prospect as if It's a Sure Thing

Remember Benjamin Franklin's sage advice—nothing is certain in this world other than death and taxes. In sales, no matter how great a particular prospect may look to you, things can change in a hurry. Even after a contract is signed, a sale can still fall through. A client once saw more than $75,000 vanish into thin air when a fire swept through the California headquarters of her prospect . . . while the contact was still being finalized by the legal team. In sales, the most volatile time is the time between when you receive a verbal go-ahead from a prospect and when the contract is received. That's when *anything* can happen. So count your deals only as 100 percent in your pipeline once you have a signed contract and a purchase order.

Adopting an Underpromise/Overdeliver Strategy

We are not big fans of the supposedly tried-and-true client relations strategy of managing expectations and then delivering results that exceed those expectations. It sends the wrong message to clients. Think about it. If you make a habit of underpromising and overdelivering, then you have established a new benchmark, a new norm and have to perform at this level each time you do business with a client. Will you always be able to meet this new expectation? Maybe not. Will your client always expect this new level of service? Absolutely yes! And if you are unable to exceed those expectations even once, then your credibility can be damaged. When dealing with a client, it's better to be specific about what you're going to do and deliver on that promise. Remember that people buy from people they trust. Trust is built by demonstrating consistent behavior over a period of time, and it's that consistency that makes buyers believe in your honesty and integrity as a salesperson.

Be careful with this one. We are *not* saying don't go the extra mile for your customer. We are saying manage the expectation carefully. Remember that above all else customers equate honesty, integrity, and trust with the consistency of your behavior. Yes, it is a fine line. Your best bet for long-term relationships is always to say what you are going to do and do it exactly the way you said you were going to.

Believing "My Success Is Unrelated to My Attitude"

Tennis pro Chris Evert was once quoted as saying:

> The thing that separates good players from great players is mental attitude. It might only make a difference of two or three points over an entire match, but how you play those key points often makes the difference between winning and losing. If the mind is strong, you can do anything you want.

Colleen's father Ted Francis (a career sales professional) is noted as saying:

> Suck it up! It's all in your head!

Both are true.

Ensuring an honest relationship with your client means starting with yourself and your own attitude.

All top-ranked salespeople share this point of view. If you ask them—as we have, repeatedly—what they do that makes them so successful, they'll answer: "It's my attitude!" Successful salespeople love what they do. They love the companies for which they work, the products and services they sell, and the clients they serve. They also take personal responsibility for ensuring that all of these points remain true. By our measure, they live by four simple rules for being honest with themselves:

Nobody Can Choose Your Attitude for You

If you're waiting for someone else to come along and motivate you, you will wait forever. Never let others take control of your thoughts. Only you can develop a better attitude for yourself. In trying times, the only way to improve your circumstances is by adopting a positive outlook. No matter what extraordinary sales techniques you learn during your career, these will fail you if you don't believe in yourself, your products, and your market.

The People around You Are a Direct Mirror of Your Attitude

Attitude is contagious. It's amazing how individuals who consistently display a poor attitude are the same people who expect their family, coworkers, friends, or employees to remain upbeat. Remember: You become who you hang out with. Think of it as the law of human magnetism.

Maintaining a Good Attitude Is Easier Than Regaining One That's Lost

If you already have a good attitude, great! Do everything you can to maintain it. Read positive books and listen to motivational tapes. Stay away from the news first thing in the morning and get rid of people in your life who are bringing you down. Sure, it's not always easy, but you will thank us for this advice when you are celebrating as the top sales rep in your company next year.

On the other hand, if you have difficulty expecting the best from yourself and others, don't give up. Remember item number one on this list—only you can choose your attitude, so it's up to you to change it.

Summing Up

- Prove your integrity with your words and actions.
- Find time to prospect every day.
- Focus on relationship building. But remember everyone's replaceable.
- All business is personal. Take it personally so you improve faster.
- Don't treat any prospect as if it's a sure thing. Nothing's certain.
- Say what you are going to do and do it exactly the way you said you were going to.
- Be honest with yourself. Be yourself. And communicate consistently with your clients.
- Work on your attitude every day. It absolutely affects your sales results.

The Hidden Costs of Communication Breakdowns

A blinding flash of the obvious: Lies and a lack of openness can cause communication breakdown, which can be costly. According to Fred Reichheld, author of *The Loyalty Effect: The Hidden Force Behind Growth, Profits and Lasting Value*, North American companies lose half of their clients every five years, half of their employees every four years, and half of their investors in less than one year. These numbers represent corporate losses that are nothing short of staggering. Why does this happen year after year? The answer is simple: communication breakdown.

Communication breakdowns can happen before a sale and after. They can happen during the sales cycle with prospects, resulting in lost deals. But they can also happen as a result of unsatisfactory after-sales service visits (or add-on sales) between salespeople and clients.

These breakdowns can cost you in terms of your overall satisfaction with your work and the satisfaction that your clients have with you and your company's services or products. Worse yet, they can damage your reputation and your ability to earn future business. However, when you're aware of the hidden costs of a communication breakdown, it's a lot easier to make smart choices about what to do to fix problems when they arise.

Seven Hidden Costs

Here's an overview of seven hidden costs of communication breakdowns. These costs are in addition to the costs that we've already discussed, such as lost sales, lost referrals, and ineffective client service. Each of these costs affects us in sales and in our daily lives.

Time

Without fail, participants in sales workshops across the United States and Canada indicate they're eager for advice and insight about time management. Sales is a time-pressure job and companies routinely put heavy pressure on salespeople to complete orders by the end of the month or by the end of each sales quarter. When pressured for time, salespeople make conscious and unconscious communications mistakes that result in dishonesty.

Sales problems or difficult clients can be a significant drain on a professional's time. As a salesperson, how much time do you normally spend thinking about particular problems you are having with clients? Do you ever have to listen to a voice-mail repeatedly or reread a document or e-mail to decipher what a client is trying to say (or not say)? Have you ever had a sale drag on longer than expected because you did not have all of the information necessary to close it? Do you feel pressure or panic at the end of a reporting period while trying to figure out how you are going to hit your numbers?

Many people would say that the highest cost of communication breakdown is wasted time.

Relationships with Clients

The value of the relationships you forge with clients can have a direct impact on whether your clients call on you again. And sales professionals everywhere should beware—we're up against a new competitor for our clients' business: the self-serve kiosk. An April 2004 article in *USA Today* suggests that North Americans are flocking to these kiosks—the self-checkout at Home Depot, the self check-in at American Airlines, and the self-pay at Exxon/Mobile. These kiosks eliminate interaction between clients and sales staff. Why is this happening? In May 2004, *Fast Company* magazine reported that self-service is taking off as a result of consumers' growing distrust of service providers. Some have lost faith in the value of relationships they used to have with salespeople. They don't trust us. This lack of faith could potentially become a job killer for our profession. Communication breakdown is having an overall impact on our relationships with clients.

Relationships with Others

Does an unresolved issue affect your relationship with colleagues, your management, or your sales support staff? Absolutely. As consultants, many salespeople tell us they hesitate to be open and honest with their colleagues for fear of being branded as blunt or difficult. When this happens, salespeople cannot find out the real causes of an unresolved issue and these accumulate to a point where people feel disconnected from others. This can come at a real cost to ongoing client service and repeat sales.

Confidence and Motivation

Salespeople are notorious for measuring and judging themselves subjectively according to the adage: "We're only as good as our last sale." Often it's tempting to judge your clients by this same measure. Some sales professionals complain that clients are dishonest with them or that they can never seem to get the whole truth out of a prospect. This can sap your confidence, encourage avoidance behavior, and undermine your motivation to succeed—all at the cost of lost leads and sales. Sometimes even making a simple cold-call can become onerous—leaving you almost paralyzed by the fear that someone will be dishonest again on the phone, even though your previous dozen calls turned into profitable new business.

Teamwork

Dr. Will Schutz, one of the founders of humanistic psychology and the creator of the Human Element®, estimated that 80 percent of work-related problems are due to a lack of open, honest communication. Is an unresolved internal or external client problem affecting the members of your team and their ability to work together? In your workplace, do salespeople withhold information and work on deals behind each other's backs? Do sales meetings drag on and fail to accomplish objectives? How is this affecting your quotas and revenue?

Staff Turnover

Why do people leave an organization? Research shows that one of the top reasons is communication issues. In fact, in some organizations poor communication can account for up to 75 percent of all employee turnover. It's worth noting that exiting staff members aren't always forthright. Not all are willing to share this reason. Instead, some will say they're leaving because of money, or compensation plans, or territory assignments—often for fear of burning their bridges behind them.

Stress

Have you ever found yourself so worried about making your next sale that you can't sleep at night or enjoy your time with family? Are you feeling fatigued or burned out? Do you feel like you've hit a wall? Have you ever squandered a weekend or a vacation because you can't stop thinking through potential opportunities or strategies that will lead to a sales breakthrough? If so, communication breakdown is costing you dearly.

We grow accustomed to living with the costs of communication breakdown. It feels like that's how it's always been. And maybe it has been—but it doesn't have to be. If you can learn to communicate honestly and openly (and you can!), then you can improve your productivity, morale, job satisfaction, ability to earn income and grow commissions, as well as your overall happiness.

Summing Up

Tackle communication breakdown and you'll get to the heart of almost any challenge you'll encounter in sales. Learning to communicate honestly and openly and to help others do the same is the answer to communication breakdown, and we'll be exploring techniques for improving two-way, open, honest communication in the coming chapters. In the next chapter we'll be discussing the important distinction between facts and assumptions and the impact that understanding can make on your sales success.

Just the Facts—How Assumptions Impact Sales

H onest, effective communication hinges on being able to make a distinction between what we know and what we think we know and applying this to our interactions with prospects, clients, colleagues, and associates. As we know, facts are the things we can observe, such as appearance, words, or actions. Our assumptions are all about thoughts, opinions, and evaluations—everything that's going on in our heads. To explain this important distinction, let's look at some examples:

- A colleague arrives for a sales meeting wearing what appears to be a new and expensive suit. You assume that he's exceeding his sales quota. Someone else might assume that he just likes to shop and can't control his spending.

- A client does not return your phone call as she promised to. You might think it's because she has chosen a competitor's product but someone else might assume the client is simply overwhelmed with work and hasn't bothered to call back because no decision has been made.

- A potential client says no, telling you the money is just not available in the budget. You may assume the client truly doesn't have the money, while another salesperson may assume the potential client just doesn't see the value in the product.

- A potential client tells you he is the decision maker, and so you assume he really is. Another salesperson may assume he's not telling the whole truth and that there may be another decision maker involved.

The trouble is that when people make assumptions, they usually don't realize they're assumptions—in other words, they think their opinions and conclusions are solid information. To make matters worse, they then make decisions based on assumptions rather than facts—only to have everyone involved suffer. The failure to distinguish between facts and assumptions can be a fatal mistake in sales.

What You Think You Know Can Hurt You

Assumptions can cloud the path to honest communication in one particularly devastating way. When we think we know the answer, we don't ask for more information. Then we go ahead and operate on our assumptions rather than the facts. Whether in sales or day-to-day living that approach can lead to big trouble. That's what happened to Tom.

Steven met Tom on an airplane, and after a customary exchange of pleasantries, they each discussed their work. After a while Tom confessed, "I wish I'd talked to you earlier." Tom was about to announce major layoffs at his company (70 to 80 percent of the workforce). A long-standing client had requested a business proposal and had also sought a proposal from one of Tom's competitors. Tom and his company submitted a 20-page proposal; the competitor submitted a 5-page proposal and won the business. Tom revealed that his team had put in the proposal what they thought the client wanted. The winning competitor's proposal included what the client actually wanted. Tom explained that the competitor had not presumed to know what the potential client might want. Tom and his team, who had been working with this client for a long time, had. They thought they knew the client well enough to assume they knew what it wanted. Tom and his team lost the business.

Lesson learned. The best salespeople operate from the position that they don't know and they listen. In short, in sales, when you think you know, it can be the beginning of the end. Watch out for people who say they know what the client wants.

Could You Be Wrong?

We don't make it through a day without making assumptions. It's a valid and important part of human thought processes. The trouble with assumptions—arriving at conclusions based on what we think we know—arises when we don't check them against verifiable facts. In business and sales, this can present a significant problem in the way we interact and communicate with clients and potential clients.

Righteousness is toxic to sales. Have you ever met someone who thinks he's always right? Or a salesperson who acts like she knows you? This is just one reason why understanding we could be wrong is so valuable.

Understanding that we may be wrong is the antidote to unchecked assumptions. And the truth is, we make assumptions constantly and many of them could be wrong. We use assumptions to fill in the blanks, especially when we first meet people. Think about it. A prospect pulls up to a meeting in a new Mercedes. This guy has money to spend, we think. But, in fact, he's drowning in the monthly payments. We look at someone's casual dress and conclude she doesn't have much money to spend, when in fact she just has never cared much about clothing or fashion. We notice someone isn't wearing a wedding ring, and we conclude he's not married. And these are just the first steps in all of our assuming. It's easy to see that our assumptions can be wrong much of the time.

Paul had recently participated in one of our sales seminars and called our office to share the results he had achieved on improving his callback rates from clients by admitting that he might be wrong.

Paul had experienced major problems in his telesales career, because many clients would not call him back. He estimated that up to 90 percent of clients were ignoring him. Paul noticed that they usually stopped calling him back after prices were discussed. He assumed that potentials were not buying from him because they had found a cheaper alternative. However, even when he lowered his price, they still didn't call back. Paul was convinced that he was right about his assessment regarding his prices. They were so high that clients were scared off. Unfortunately, Paul's boss was not convinced of this theory, and he concluded that Paul lacked performance skills and initiative. He refused to authorize any more price discounts. Paul then began to blame the company and his boss for his poor performance.

After our session, Paul decided to accept the idea that he just might be wrong—that maybe prices weren't the issue after all. He returned to the office and started calling clients, leaving a very specific voice mail: "I notice that you have been difficult to reach, and I suspect it's either because you are worried that our prices are too high, or because your project is on hold. Either reason is okay. Please call me at (we won't disclose Paul's number even though we're quite sure he'd love to pitch to you!) so that we can determine the next steps—if there are any—together."

The end result of Paul's efforts: his callbacks increased more than 80 percent and his sales rocketed by 30 percent. As soon as his clients understood that Paul really cared and was willing to accept their decision, they wanted to talk. When they called back, they were willing to reciprocate his willingness to listen and to care. In addition, Paul found new business in many deals that had been previously stalled.

Next, he applied his newfound winning method to his interaction with staff and other sales associates. He asked more questions and checked the facts before making decisions. When someone gave him advice, he would listen carefully and remain open-minded to the possibility that the other person just might have a good point. This simple technique put his career back on track and improved his performance. It put Paul within striking range of becoming a top 20 percent performer in his organization—all within a six-month period.

And this success simply came from discovering and accepting that he might be wrong!

In business and sales, people observe—and think they see—plenty of things they assume to be true. Most of these will remain unspoken, even the assumptions that are incorrect or misunderstood. The trick is to examine your assumptions and question them. Go to the source. Above all, don't let yourself and your sales success be held back by unbridled assuming.

Another form of trouble comes from experience with our own products and services. As salespeople become more and more experienced with their company or product, they can actually become less and less effective. You would expect the opposite to be true, but as consultants, we've witnessed this phenomenon repeatedly.

Why Does This Happen?

The answer is a matter of human nature. When we become intimately familiar with something, we begin to mistakenly assume that the client understands what we're talking about. Moreover, we sometimes assume that a client's problems are the same as those we've dealt with before. For example, suppose in the past a client complained about price and ended up being a very difficult person to deal with. The next time we're faced with a potential client who makes similar complaints about pricing, we may think, "Here we go again" and assume we're dealing with another very difficult person. If we go along with that assumption, we may develop an attitude or even give up and not pursue the opportunity. A less experienced salesperson may encounter those same questions about pricing and instead be pleasantly persistent and probe to find out what is going on. If the client was simply trying to get the best price, the less experienced salesperson may win the business after demonstrating why the product is such a great value. This situation is not uncommon and explains why new salespeople or competitors can often win business against the incumbent.

To Make Matters Worse . . .

As if the news about assumptions and our human tendency to fill in the blanks with wrong information wasn't enough, there are a few additional factors that compound this problem of facts versus assumptions: people love to be right, our history can color our assumptions (and we don't even realize it), and people love to associate with other people just like them. Let's take a quick look at each of these issues.

People Love to Be Right

People love to be right—it's human nature. Often, people will even search for things, even a gut feeling, to validate an assumption. In doing so, they often miss facts that might point to a different conclusion about a person, place, or thing. To compound the problem, we tend to remember only the times we're right and conveniently forget the times we're wrong.

People look for and remember the evidence that supports their assumptions. Apply this fact to our sales environment: those we sell to and communicate with only see what they want to see and what they perceive to be the truth. As salespeople, we often do the same.

No wonder many salespeople continue to have difficulties closing their sales and have conflicts with their clients! They are likely the same people who think that they are always right, but we know that no one is always right and that our assumptions are frequently wrong.

This is why feedback is so important. It gives people an opportunity to verbalize what they think—to say what they believe to be true. Make no mistake about it: The truth hurts at times. But it beats the alternative in which people, groups, or entire organizations go on making bad decisions based on inaccurate or incomplete facts.

Think of it this way: Being wrong is an opportunity. We can ask the client why we lost the business and use that information to gain—and keep—future business. In the future you may even get that client back due to the relationship you develop by going back to him and asking for the truth. We know someone who eventually won back a 20 million dollar piece of business by doing something just like this.

Our research suggests that the most confident salespeople are seldom interested in playing the blame game—they want solutions. Salespeople who have a hard time admitting they might be wrong (or that they're sorry) tend to be, at best, the mediocre performers in an organization.

Personal History Colors Assumptions

Your own history has a powerful effect on what you imagine to be true. When Steven realized this, it had a profound impact on his ability to sell and to choose the career path that was right for him.

> At the age of three I was unable to speak correctly. I could just mumble a few words, and a doctor advised my mother to put me in a class for "slow" children. She refused and took me to other doctors, who discovered multiple ear infections that were affecting my hearing and therefore my ability to communicate. A series of operations and three years of speech therapy corrected the problem, and no one has been able to shut me up since!
>
> Yet I came out of that early childhood experience believing I was stupid. I compensated by studying hard and came out in the top 1 percent of my college class and still I thought I was stupid. I rationalized that the only reason I did so well was because I studied harder than the other students. All of this affected my attitude, which in turn affected my sales ability (as we discussed previously). I never liked or believed in what I was selling until I got involved with personal development. Then I dealt with my own insecurities and became a believer . . . and voilà . . . I was able to sell.

We allow our personal history to dictate not just how we feel about ourselves but what we imagine about others. Our history influences the way we view the facts. It colors our assumptions, influences the way we interact with others, and skews our interpretation of data, which then affects sales. In short, our history distorts the data that we receive.

If you've hit a wall with sales, you might take some time to examine your deep-seated assumptions about yourself and your abilities. That could make all the difference. How did you grow up? What kind of assumptions have you developed about yourself? What kind of assumptions have you developed about others? About money? We know people whose trouble with sales is rooted in these sorts of issues—their assumptions about money, about their own likeability, and so forth. In our experience these sorts of assumptions can have a strong effect on sales success—or the lack thereof.

We Associate with People Who Think Like Us

A major factor that compounds the problem with assumptions is that we tend to associate with people who think like us. So if Bill makes an assumption about a client or potential client, that assumption will likely be affirmed by Bill's colleagues, because he spends the most time with the coworkers who think like he does.

This fact of human nature can lead to huge miscalculations with clients and potential clients. If you only associate with those people who always share the same opinions as you, be careful. Nobody is right as often as they think they are.

Reversing the Mistake of Assuming

Once we accept that there's a danger in assuming we're right all the time, the next step is to take action to reverse our mistakes. That starts with a change of mindset. Does it really matter that you don't understand intuitively what your client or prospect wants? It's worth remembering that people don't always buy for the reasons we think they do. People have their own reasons. So how can you best find out what motivates each new prospect to buy? There's really only one way: by asking questions first in an honest two-way conversation and then adjusting and providing the appropriate information.

Not everyone likes to recognize the dangers of being right. We've encountered more than one skeptic. Here's an example of a persistent doubter who wanted tips to help boost her sales performance.

Sandy was an experienced telesales rep who worked in Philadel-phia and had clients all over the West Coast of the United States. She was what some might affectionately call a "fast talker"— always excited and passionate about the products she sold. She was also an expert in her field and never missed an opportunity to tell her clients all about it. While Sandy had always achieved her sales targets through a combination of hard work and persistence, she had never been able to make the breakthrough that would help her exceed her goals on a consistent basis.

Sandy always sold her products the same way, with the same messages, regardless of the client. Because of the depth of her knowledge, she was convinced she knew exactly why people needed her products . . . and she wasn't afraid to remind them of this! One day on a coaching call, Lisa mentioned that she had a bad cold and that her sore throat was making it difficult to talk. Then she said something quite revealing: "For the past week I've had such low energy levels that I haven't wanted to talk to my clients. Instead, I've been asking the questions, and letting them talk to me . . . and I've been amazed at some of the reasons I'm hearing about why people are buying our products. I would never have thought to sell them that way. In fact, most of our clients are using the products in ways I would never have thought possible."

Armed with this new insight, Sandy was able, for the first time, to push her sales to 20 percent over quota. It's a simple illustration, but it shows how one little change in business habits can reap some pretty surprising rewards.

Salespeople Who Think They Know Best

There's no better way to reevaluate a situation than by consid-ering it from someone else's perspective. Put yourself in your client's shoes for a moment. Would you want to deal with a salesperson who thought he knew what was best for you?

Consider Sandy's experience in the previous example. She had been right much less than half of the time in her assumptions about what her clients wanted, and this was clearly affecting her ability to close sales. Her change of behavior—while it was first brought on by a cold—prompted her to reconsider her habits. She decided she needed to continue asking questions and to listen carefully to the clients' reasons for buying instead of telling them her own.

In fact, using the honest communication tools she had learned, Sandy continued to initiate conversations with prospects who seemed to be turning to the competition. She actively sought out their advice and asked questions about how they could make the product work for them. Sales increased.

In sales, the better we understand that we're often mistaken, the more open-minded we will be in our interactions, and the better we will be able to communicate our point of view.

Here's an example of this approach:

"I noticed that we have not talked since I sent the proposal. I am thinking that maybe you didn't like the price, or that the information wasn't comprehensive enough. Maybe I am off-base. What are your thoughts about the proposal?"

It is possible to gain confidence from learning to ask questions and uncovering the facts rather than living with the false confidence of believing we're always right. Experience doesn't mean we're right all the time; it means we have a more highly developed ability to ask better questions.

Can you imagine if we all lived this way? If everyone around us was open to being wrong? If we all gave our clients and others the benefit of the doubt more often? If everyone was willing to say what needs to be said and willing to hear how we could better work together? In such a world people wouldn't hide behind e-mail. They would pick up the phone and have a two-way, open, honest conversation. Great gains can be made in our ability to have honest communication when we learn to accept the idea that we could be wrong and examine our assumptions.

Benefits to Examining Assumptions

Learning to distinguish between assumption and fact can pay important dividends in our professional and personal lives. Let's look at some specific ways this simple distinction can affect the sales success of an organization.

Uncover Hidden Sales Opportunities

Sales opportunities are lost when ideas from people on the front lines (salespeople, client service reps, as well as technical people) don't make it up to the top of the decision-making chain. Did you know that the Big Mac was an idea from a franchisee—not from McDonald's headquarters? Where would our country—this world—be without the Big Mac? (Wait, don't answer that!)

Those out in the field are closer to the clients. This enables them to come up with valuable ideas that might never be generated at corporate headquarters. But many of those great ideas never get passed along to those in a position to make them happen. When we ask people why they don't forward their big ideas, they say it's because they assume they won't get the credit or that it's not worth the effort. They assume their idea won't be taken seriously or ever come to fruition. This is stunning because it happens so often.

What big idea have you chosen not to pass along? What sales opportunities is your organization missing out on? What assumptions are holding you and your organization back?

If you're in a position to make things happen in your organization, ask yourself how many sales opportunities and ideas you hear about on a weekly basis. If it's few to none, we can guarantee that the ideas are out there. You need to facilitate the free flow of ideas throughout your organization. Internal feedback should be a highly valued channel for sales opportunities.

There is another set of assumptions that may be impacting your organization's sales opportunities—and that's the assumptions of your clients. One complaint that we frequently hear is the way clients assume that a company they've been working with doesn't have the particular product or service that they need. They make assumptions about your capabilities and don't even ask if you can fulfill a new need that has developed. For instance, when John needed a web site for his start-up business, he contacted a firm that does web design. They did a great web site for him, but when he needed some print advertising, John went elsewhere because he assumed the web design firm doesn't do print advertising. It does.

Educating clients about all of your products and services and informing them of new products and services as they roll out is the way to combat these crippling assumptions. It pays to be persistent in managing client assumptions and expectations, and that persistence will uncover new sales opportunities.

Increase Individual Initiative and Persistence

Another benefit to examining assumptions is that it can increase your initiative and persistence. Some people don't get a return call and assume that the potential client is not interested. Perhaps they're not. But that's an assumption, not a fact. Maybe other things have come up and it's a bad time. Maybe it was assigned to someone else. Who knows?

How we interpret the facts has everything to do with whether we'll take more initiative and be persistent. Great salespeople know that for every no, they may be getting closer to a yes. In sales and in life, imagined assumptions can cripple us if we're not careful. They can not only affect our sales and how we interact with others, they can also significantly influence our careers. That's what happened to Kevin.

Kevin seemed to have stopped taking the initiative for new marketing ideas and business development. Several months earlier, Kevin's boss, Susan, had told him he was in line to be promoted as the new sales director for the region. But months passed without a follow-up discussion about the promotion. Kevin began to imagine that his boss had changed her mind. In retaliation, he stopped assuming a leadership role, ceased all initiatives, and performed only the necessary tasks associated with his position.

After a lengthy period of feeling resentful, Kevin sought out and found a new job. In his exit interview with Susan, he confronted her about being overlooked for the position. He maintained that this demonstrated a lack of respect for his work and that was why he was leaving the company. Susan was genuinely surprised and said she would have promoted him a long time ago, but had assumed he didn't want the promotion because of the extra hours it required. She explained that she had noticed how Kevin had earlier complained about working long hours and not having time enough for his family. Later, Kevin's frustration appeared to Susan to be a lack of initiative.

A short conversation could have prevented this misunderstanding. Instead, valuable resources went untapped, hard feelings were harbored, and everyone lost something.

Motivate a Sales Force

Leaders will often design rewards for their teams based on what motivates them personally. Shouldn't the reward be designed based on what motivates the team? A reward can be a great motivator, but there are perils in giving rewards that you think people will want. Consider the following example:

Recently during a coaching session, Brian, the sales director of an international software company, shared an example of how he attempted to motivate a series of teams. The end of the fiscal year was fast approaching and his teams were dangerously close to not hitting their revenue targets. To get things back on track, Brian promised each team that its members would be treated to a company-sponsored ski trip if the sales numbers were met. Sales started to grow everywhere, except for one team on the West Coast. Brian reminded this team about the ski trip, hoping to increase their productivity, but to no avail. Later, the leader of the West Coast team gave him an insight into what went wrong: None of the team members were enticed by the skiing offer because none could ski very well . . . and no one owned the equipment required to participate in the trip.

By attempting to use what he imagined would be a good motivator for everyone, Brian accomplished the opposite with his West Coast team. Examining his assumptions would have enabled him to more successfully motivate all the teams.

Increase Client Feedback, Service, and Loyalty

When consulting with clients, we often observe salespeople avoiding or refusing to deal with a problem, because they assume that addressing it could anger a client and send them to the competition. In these situations, we're inclined to ask whether this behavior creates client-service issues or disloyal clients down the road.

We often observe sales managers or sales teams wrongly concluding that a client offering negative feedback is simply a troublemaker or a problem client. Worse still, sales teams will make a concerted effort to avoid communicating with that client. That's when trouble ensues. When an organization ignores its clients, it has less factual information to rely on. The client, in turn, is in the same situation. With both parties relying on their opinions and assumptions to guide them instead of the facts, a bad situation can easily become worse.

Consider the following example in which a salesperson made promises that turned out to be too good to be true.

A client-service team at a software company was dealing with an error in its software that a client had complained about. The team sensed there was no satisfactory answer to the problem. The development team indicated that it would take more than nine months to fix it. The client-service team assumed that the client wanted the problem fixed immediately and that it would be unhappy to hear this news. Weeks passed. The client-service team delayed calling the client back. Not surprisingly, the client became angry and imagined that the company didn't care about its concerns. Finally, the client called and demanded to know what was going on.

In the end, this team was responsible for losing the client to the competition because of a perceived notion that the company was indifferent to the client's needs. If the client-service team had chosen to double-check what it had imagined to be true and had provided upfront, honest answers, it would have solved the matter to everyone's satisfaction.

Keep this statistic in mind: 67 percent of lost business each year is lost because of clients who imagine that their service provider is indifferent to their needs and wants. We're not saying that you, as the service providers *are* indifferent, just that your clients imagine you are. Their perception leads them to leave. That's a staggering percentage of clients leaving for the same reason! And it's especially difficult to accept when mistaken assumptions may be at the root of the problem. Without honest communication, an organization cannot understand the true needs and wants of its clients.

A Golden Opportunity: Uncovering the Real Decision Makers

When you first get in touch with a potential client, you have a golden opportunity to examine assumptions. Have you ever hesitated to ask whether your prospect was the real decision maker for a project, worried that you might offend him if he wasn't? People often say they make the decisions when they really don't. By the same token, don't assume someone is the decision maker just because of a job title. To complicate matters further, someone may technically be the decision maker but may actually rely on an assistant in such matters.

Many sales books provide advice for circumventing the gatekeeper, but in doing that you may offend the very person who can influence the decision-making process. Consider leveraging the gatekeeper to help you gain access to the decision maker more quickly. One way to get to the heart of the matter without offending your contact is to ask a more open-ended question. Rather than asking, *"Are you the decision maker?"* ask, *"How do decisions get made in your organization?"* or *"The last time a decision was made to_____ how did you go about it?"*

For more ideas on how to leverage the gatekeeper and get to the real decision maker, please visit www.honestysells.com and visit the resources section. Look for the article called "Leveraging gatekeepers for sales success."

You may also need to get beyond your assumptions if you're taking over a territory and you're being debriefed by the former salesperson. Be careful not to assume that everything the former salesperson tells you in the debriefing is the truth. If the individual bad-mouths particular clients, it's best to discard those opinions. Get to know the territory and your clients yourself. Don't avoid the clients that the previous salesperson disliked. By the way, if clients sense they're a low priority, they'll feel dissatisfied. If you avoid a client based on the previous salesperson's assessment, a good client may turn into a difficult one!

No Means . . . I Don't Know

Perhaps the most important assumption that salespeople need to check in with is the idea that no means no. Even kids know that's not true. They're the masters at hearing the possibility behind the word no; so are good salespeople. When a potential client says no, it's time for a new approach. When someone says no, it's always relevant to ask this question: "*Under what circumstances would you change your mind?*"

If a client provides a reason for saying no, the key is to not assume that the initial objection is the real objection. We should always seize the opportunity to ask more questions. If money is the objection, it's a good chance to look deeper. When people say money is the problem, they often mean that value is. Just think of yourself in everyday life. You may tell someone you can't afford something but then turn around and buy something else that costs even more.

Saying no because of financial issues sounds like a definitive reason for an answer of no, and it can actually mask a variety of reasons. Perhaps the client hasn't had enough time to think your proposal through, perhaps he doesn't see the value, or perhaps his boss never wanted to go with your company. If you don't check in and go deeper, you won't know. Don't ever assume that no means no. In Colleen's previous sales

careers she sold records management software to the oil industry. She shares the following:

> A large potential client had said no to a $350,000 project we
> proposed and I was dumbfounded. My team had done every-
> thing right and built the proposal exactly to meet the needs of
> the prospect. After weeks of examining the project our pros-
> pect said no, and we discovered it was because she did not
> have the money in her budget.
>
> I decided to ask some questions to confirm my assumptions:
>
> - How much money was in your budget?
> - When does your budget cycle end and start?
> - When will you have additional money?
>
> What I discovered was:
>
> - They had $300,000 in their budget.
> - Their budget cycle ended March 31 and started again
>   April 1 *and*
> - They would have additional money to spend April 1.
>
> Considering it was March 15 when we had this conversa-
> tion, I was able to offer a new solution: Split the project in
> two and spend $300,000 in March and the remaining $50,000
> in April.
>
> The client accepted and was pleased we could get started
> right away. I was pleased because we secured the deal quickly,
> without negotiation and discounting.

Getting Out of Voice Mail Jail

Making suggestions and checking assumptions is a practice
that works well for those who are eager to get past voice mail
and get to prospects and clients. Let's look at how making suggestions and going beyond assumptions can help on a series of

typical prospecting calls. As a side note, our clients who use this approach are having similar results to Jerry who told us that *"this approach to voice mail has increased my callback rates up to 80 percent."* We know you can have these results too, so you might want to get a pen out and take notes in the margin now.

The First Call

> Elaine, this is Dave Smith from Smith & Company. I was talking to (offer a name or referral) yesterday who asked that I call you. Sorry I missed you today. I promise to reach you again on (date) and (time).

Tip: Make sure your tone is soft, nonthreatening, and friendly. You don't want to sound like a radio ad for a furniture liquidator. Plus, it's critical that you do call back exactly on the date and time that you say. Yes! We are suggesting you *not* leave your phone number. Why? Because we want you to stand out not blend in with other sales reps. While others are begging and cajoling clients and prospects for a return call you are taking matters into your own hands and telling the client not to worry; the client can trust you to do all the work.

The Follow-Up

> Hi, Elaine. This is Dave Smith from Smith & Company calling because I promised to call you back today and I'm sorry we missed each other. (Referral source) was hoping that we would be able to connect. I'll try you again on (date) and (time).

Tip: Again, it's critical that you call back exactly when you said you would. Anything else would result in your being less than honest and risk losing your prospect's confidence. Our clients find that up to 50 percent of all clients and prospects are waiting for their calls on this second attempt so don't be surprised if they pick up the phone!

One Last Try

> Hi Elaine. This is Dave at Smith & Company calling because I promised to reach you today. Sorry I missed you. I notice that you have been difficult to reach this week and I suspect it's because you're either swamped at work, you are not interested in the work that we do, or I've been wrong at picking the times you might be at your desk. Either is okay. You can reach me at 111-1111 to let me know how you would like to proceed. I promised (referral source) I would let (him/her) know the outcome of our conversation and if I don't hear from you in a couple weeks I will call you on (date) and (time).

Tip: This approach works because it builds trust by being nonthreatening, honest, and friendly—essential attributes of a successful salesperson. It also works because it means you have shifted your focus from trying to make a sale to trying to start a conversation. And it works because you're checking in about your assumptions and attempting to get the facts. In doing this, you give your prospect the expectation that you can be trusted to keep your word, and you begin to build rapport—crucial to winning new business.

What You Can Do

Learning to keep your assumptions in check is a simple skill to acquire, but applying it consistently to your work takes effort. While this skill can provide you with a very important reward—being able to sell more in less time—many sales professionals still don't take the time to learn how to incorporate this into their sales repertoire.

Remember, the more we understand that we may be wrong, the more success we'll have in sales because that understanding will drive us to ask more questions. The more questions we ask, the more facts we obtain. And the more facts we have, the better the decisions. The better the decisions, the more sales we'll make. The key is to ask the questions from the belief that your assumptions really might be incorrect. That way you'll listen closely for the answers, and your sales will benefit. Throughout the sales process, continue to check your assumptions.

Let's look at a sales scenario that would have benefited from the salesperson checking in with the client by checking assumptions and asking a few more questions.

As a software sales representative, Kathleen was told by one of her prospects that the firm's procurement and legal teams would have to first review the software provider's licensing agreement and contract before any deal could be finalized. This process would start once the prospect had chosen to buy from Kathleen's company. Assuming that the prospect's team would accept the contracts and agreements at face value and would not be able to cancel the sale, she waited until the very last minute to submit the licensing agreements for review. The prospect had waited (impatiently) to install the software and Kathleen had to wait to invoice the legal and procurement teams. Three months passed and still no contract. Both sides were still arguing over the licensing agreement!

Had Kathleen checked her assumptions when her prospect first mentioned the involvement of legal and procurement staff, the discussion with the client might have sounded like this: "I notice you mentioned that legal and purchasing will need to be involved, and I imagine this could either be a long process that could delay the implementation, or that they normally accept vendors' agreements as is. What do you think is more likely to happen?'' That question might have drawn out the truth that vendors' agreements were rarely taken at face value. That would have given Kathleen important facts with which to make better decisions (perhaps to suggest they start the review process in parallel with finishing the sale).

There's a sad footnote to this example. During the three months of negotiations and delay, the potential client's office was hit by a tornado, destroying the building. All paperwork was lost. The sale never closed.

Summing Up

The ability to accept that you may be wrong, examine your assumptions, and check in and ask more questions is an essential component of honest communication. It's an ability that will serve you well throughout the sales process and result in greater understanding and, in the long term, greater sales success. In this chapter, we have covered many examples in which people hurt their credibility and undermined their own potential simply by not keeping their assumptions in check. It's an indispensable skill to have—one that will serve you well in your career whether you're an ambitious junior sales associate or a seasoned vice president of sales for a Fortune 500 company.

We've illustrated that there's something inherently ironic about what it takes to be a successful, top-ranked, sales associate. Bucking conventional assumptions (and the natural tendency that so many of us have) about the need to be right all the time is step one. In sales, the path to success and happiness demands that you accept that you might be wrong. Accepting the notion of being wrong doesn't have to lead to a crisis of confidence. Instead you can build your self-esteem on the basis of accepting that you might be wrong, discovering the truth, moving beyond blame, and implementing real solutions.

There is no magic behind what we've recommended in this chapter. But let's be clear. Applying this knowledge—that you might be wrong and need to take the appropriate steps—requires a lot of effort . . . and practice. In Chapter 7, we'll look at how the next key—being honest with yourself—is a skill that extends in all directions of a salesperson's professional and personal life.

Be a Life Giver

S alespeople generally fall into one of two categories: They're either Life Suckers or Life Givers. Life Suckers blame others for their actions and results, whereas Life Givers take responsibility and ownership for their actions and get results. Those who are always looking for solutions to challenges are salespeople with an agent—or ownership— attitude. They embrace the fact that their jobs—our jobs!— require that they act responsibly. Rather than wasting time assigning blame, they move forward by creating solutions.

You are an adult. Nobody makes adults think or do anything. You are responsible for your actions, your thoughts, opinions, assumptions, and conclusions. They belong to you. You choose to think or act a certain way. Taking responsibility is a matter of choice. So, when you say, "the client stressed me out," "the prospect pressured me," or "my manager made me do this"— what you are really saying is that others control you. It's as if you expect people to believe that some kind of "others" phantom crept into your body and took control of what you think and do. Get over it! Life does not imitate a Hollywood horror film. It's up to each of us to choose how we feel and act.

As a side note—as consultants we are regularly asked to evaluate talent on a sales team. We find there are telltale signs of failure. One critical sign is the answer to this question:

Tell me about your last loss. What happened? A sales rep who makes excuses—"*it's shipping's fault we lost the deal*"—is doomed to fail. A sales rep who takes ownership—"*I should have qualified the lead better*" is destined for greatness. Our accuracy at determining successful versus unsuccessful reps is 95 percent with this one question.

Sure, bad things can happen—and they happen even to the best salespeople. None of us can choose or control every event that occurs in our lives, especially the ones that affect our business. Have you ever lost a sale to a prospect that was acquired before you had the contract signed? We have. Have you ever had a sale to a government department wind up in limbo because of an unexpected spending freeze imposed while you were in final negotiations? We have. These are examples of situations that as salespeople we can't control; however, we can always choose how we respond to and deal with these events.

Consider the conduct expected of first-year cadets at military colleges across North America. They are only allowed to respond to their instructors in one of three ways: "Yes sir," "No sir," and "No excuses, sir!" If a cadet fails to complete an assignment (and the circumstances are deemed irrelevant), the cadet must assume responsibility by stating, "No excuses, sir!" The purpose here is to create an ownership attitude. A leadership attitude. It's that kind of self-discipline and ownership that will serve you well in your career.

Here are four exercises that you can try every day to make sure you are a Life Giver.

Associate Only with Life Givers

You have complete control over the people with whom you spend your time, so choose wisely. Being around positive people will improve your outlook and your attitude. Our client Jim calls this the Rule of Lunch:

> Whenever I have lunch with someone and I feel worse off when I get back to the office, I never have lunch with that person again. On the other hand, if I come back to the office

feeling invigorated, I try to schedule lunch or coffee with the person as often as I can!

Jim's got it right. You become who you hang out with. So pick all your associates carefully. Friends, clients, and family.

Laugh, Learn, and Take Responsibility

In baseball, you're a candidate for the Hall of Fame if you regularly bat 500. Top goalies have a goals against average of greater than 1. And except for Lance Armstrong, even the highest paid golfers, race car drivers, and cyclists don't win all the tournaments, games, or races they enter. Yet the majority of salespeople still get frustrated when they can't close every piece of business that comes their way.

Top performers know different.

Let's face it—even the best salespeople have lost far more business over the years than they've won. And that's okay. But while the rest of us whine, complain, or blame everyone else we can think of, the top 10 percent of salespeople continue to be inherently optimistic regardless of whether they "win" or "lose." Instead of attempting to pass the buck, they take full responsibility for their losses, never blame others, and always try to learn from their mistakes. Then they move on to other serious prospects as quickly as they can.

When something bad happens—and it does to everyone—look for the good in it and take full responsibility for the bad. Those salespeople who aren't afraid to admit when they're wrong are the same ones who comprise the ranks of the top performers (which we discuss throughout this book). Clients don't have time for mistakes and blame. Being honest makes you more trustworthy and earns you something that's truly invaluable: a reputation for integrity. So the next time you make a mistake, ask yourself what you can learn from it. Then take that lesson and use it.

Train Your Mind for Success by Achieving a Realizable Goal Every Day

People often get into a negative rut because they feel they aren't making progress. If that sounds familiar, then try setting a small but achievable goal for yourself every day. Make a list. Write down each goal, and when you've achieved each one, cross it off. Before too long you'll have a pattern of successful achievement that will help you develop a pattern of positive thinking.

Actions Speak Louder Than Words

Whether we like it or not, people don't only pay attention to what we're saying when they're making a decision whether to trust us. They also judge us by how we say things, and especially by how we act.

We know—you're screaming right now, *"That's not fair, I was always taught not to judge a book by its cover, and others shouldn't either!"* You're right; it's not fair. Unfortunately, it's still the way the vast majority of people operate when deciding whether to trust others around them. Given that this fact of life isn't about to go away, why not learn to use it to prove your honesty?

Top performers know that they have to be compassionate not only in their words, but also in their nonverbal communication. This means making eye contact, shaking your prospect's hand, taking notes to prove you're interested, watching that your tone is consistent with what you really mean, and respecting your customers enough to dress appropriately for a meeting.

Yes, this is all Basic Sales 101. And sure, sometimes clients do accuse us of being elementary. Not the successful ones though. As simple as this honesty strategy sounds to implement, the sad truth is that 80 percent of the salespeople we coach do not pay attention to basic nonverbal communication.

We've seen salespeople who constantly look over the shoulders of their prospects to see if someone more important is walking by. We've witnessed salespeople looking at the floor or their presentation slides during multimillion dollar sales presentations rather than at their prospects. We've watched salespeople who answer their cell phones during sales calls, show up late for meetings, don't shake hands, or wear old, scuffed-up shoes. All these actions negatively affect your relationship with the prospect and can make you seem dishonest.

Taking care of nonverbal communication is something that top performers practice every day, because they know that it directly affects the rapport and trust they build with their prospects. In the long run, it is honesty that builds rapport, rapport that leads to trust, and trust that leads to winning a customer for life.

Be Likable

How often have you thought, based merely on observation, that someone was a loser? Like it or not, most humans are prone to prejudice. We form our opinions about others before we even know them, talk to them, or interact with them. Sorry, we can't teach you how to change this fact about human interaction; we can only teach you how to use this human tendency for prejudice to your advantage. In a couple words: Be likable.

Sales success is about focusing on basics. Never mind the elaborate "selling systems" or prefab scripts that are out there. The single most important thing you can do to improve your sales performance in any kind of organization is this: be nice to people.

Nice leads to like. Like leads to trust. Trust leads to a sale.

What is nice?

By "nice" we don't just mean that you need to be nice in a small way (you know . . . to always remember your manners just like Mom taught you). What we mean is that it's important to be nice in a big way—in a way that can make a difference in the lives of others.

There are millions of little things that each of us can do every day to be nice to others. From remembering birthdays to sending thank-you cards, from doing little extras for others to sending chocolates or flowers to someone you're thinking of—when you make a point of being nice, you play a role in the happiness of others. And just as important, you help shape how others see you.

Think of how you felt the last time you received an unexpected card from a friend or someone you work with. It's a good feeling, right? And it means a lot when you know that someone has taken the time to think about you. It says that someone cares about you and wants you to be happy.

At a conference we interviewed a top 1 percent performer for a large chemical company. Bill was the number one sales rep for his company three years running. When asked to what he attributed his success, this is what he said:

> The guys who hit quota know the client's birthday. The guys in the top 10 percent know the client's wife's birthday. I know the client's dog's birthday.

The lesson: Bill is nice. Bill is a Life Giver. Bill is a top performer.

The Way You Do the Things You Do

Of course when it's just a kind gesture or two, being nice doesn't take much effort at all. But making a habit of it means that a bit more thinking has to go into what you're doing. Getting good—really good—at being nice means you have to keep an eye on the things you do on a regular basis.

Here are three tips to keep in mind.

First, be consistent. If you want to be the person who always remembers everyone's birthday, it's not going to be enough to remember just once and then never again. By being consistent, you demonstrate to people that you're not being nice simply because you woke up one morning in a great mood. You're showing that this is something you do as a matter of practice . . . because you really care. Trust is built through consistent behavior over time.

Second, be prompt. Don't wait a month before sending out thank-you cards after hosting or attending that great event. Do something while the memory and the good feelings are still fresh in everyone's minds. You're sending a powerful message to people about what matters to you in your life.

Third, be thoughtful. This is where your creativity and attention to detail can help you really stand out. Remember that there are no limits to how much you can care for others. Recently we interviewed a top salesperson and asked her what set her apart from everyone else in her business. *"I genuinely love people and I like showing how much I appreciate them,"* she explained. *"There are plenty who remember to send out a birthday card to a friend or client, but I'll bet I'm the only one who thinks to also send out an anniversary card to the couple!"*

Just a Little of the Human Touch

Being nice is all about getting in touch with the human element of what we do in life. And as obvious as it may seem, the importance of being nice is, like a lot of basics, something that a lot of people overlook or underestimate. And yet it's timeless advice. Go back and look at what people like Zig Ziglar and Tom Hopkins were teaching 40 years ago. They recognized, as we do, that there is immense potential in the power of goodwill and kindness. And that applies not just to our personal relationships, but to our business ones, too.

Remember that buying is a very personal, emotional decision. When buyers have a choice, they'll choose to do business with the person they like and trust the most. That's what's missing in the process approach to sales—and that's why adopters of that approach tend to wind up disappointed.

The process approach to sales tells people to behave the same way in front of every client—start with step one, then proceed to step two, then step three. There's no room for, well, the niceties of life. Instead, it assumes that buyer behavior can be changed by force. And that's how buyers and sellers get out of sync.

On the other hand, making a habit of being nice has its own modest requirements—you need to invest some time listening to and thinking about others.

But it pays dividends in all kinds of ways that all those sales approaches simply cannot touch! Not only does it help make you a better person and help shape the lives of others, being nice can also influence the bottom line of your organization.

Consider the firsthand experience of Linda Kaplan Thaler and Robin Korval, the authors of *The Power of Nice: How to Conquer the Business World with Kindness.* "*In less than a decade, we built the Kaplan Thaler Group into a powerhouse in* *advertising with close to $1 billion in billings. . . . Our success was won not with pitchforks and spears, but with flowers and chocolates . . . (and) smiles and compliments."*

By investing a little in the power of being nice—listening compassionately to others and tending to their needs—you can make an amazing difference in your life and in the lives of others. You create honest and profitable relationships. Just as the Dalai Lama sagely prescribes: "If you want others to be happy, practice compassion. If you want to be happy, practice compassion." We agree and also add that if you want to be successful (and rich) in sales, practice compassion.

Summing Up

Take ownership of your behavior and assumptions. Remember, no one made you come up with those thoughts, opinions, assumptions, and conclusions; and only you can steer things right. The top 10 percent of salespeople ensure that clients feel better after interacting with them. Not worse. In doing so they guarantee that every communication is focused on enhancing likability, developing trust, and ensuring a long-term mutually profitable relationship.

Whether you're looking to improve your personal relationships or your record as a sales professional, concentrate on fine-tuning this important basic—be nice! By doing so, happiness and profits will find you.

Getting the Truth from Everyone

W e train and condition clients to treat us the way we want to be treated.

Consider, for example, the use of sales and discounts. How often do you hold yourself true to your word when you offer someone a limited-time discount? It's a time-honored tradition to offer a prospect a discount on a sale when nearing month's end, as an incentive to buy now rather than later. And it comes with an implicit threat:

> I can only offer you this discount if you buy before April 30th; after that, it's back to full price.

But let's face facts: If that prospect calls back on May 5th demanding the discounted price, you are very likely to give it to them. This behavior conditions clients and establishes a precedent that they'll anticipate again and again, seeing your limited-time offer as anything but limited. They will begin to expect that a lower price is something they can demand all the time.

Another way to inadvertently train clients and team members is to avoid making any kind of response at all to undesirable behavior—to remain silent. For example:

A banker—let's call him John—was having problems with his loans officers in the branch. When they did something that he didn't like—like forgetting to ask for referrals—John wouldn't say anything, hoping that his silence would make a point. Instead, it had the opposite effect—employees kept repeating the undesirable behavior.

Likewise, if a client yells at us and we don't say anything, we've just rewarded this person's behavior; our lack of reaction signals that it's okay to treat us that way. Clients notice silence; and they often interpret it as agreement or consent when, in fact, it's meant to convey disagreement. That's why many salespeople who have an aversion to conflict often find themselves knee-deep in one, despite their best efforts.

We can even train ourselves—as well as others—to deny the truth. Have you ever intentionally arrived late for a company sales meeting because you knew from past experience that it wouldn't start on time? If you're nodding your head in agreement, congratulations; the person who chairs those meetings (maybe your sales manager?) has trained you and the teams. Your behavior has changed because of an expected outcome.

Take It Personally! How to Accept—and Benefit from—Criticism

Look at your own sales habits. How are you training your manager to deal with you? What are you teaching your clients to do? For example, if you ask your manager to be honest with you and subsequently become defensive when he is—what happens? Your action (or reaction) might train someone to be dishonest with you, as it did in the following scenario:

Bill had a sales manager who was lying to him repeatedly. While he kept demanding that the manager tell him the truth, it never seemed to work. After discussing the matter with us, Bill spoke to the sales manager and asked him: "What is it about me that makes you feel uncomfortable about telling me the truth?" The answers to this question gave Bill some important insights about what he could do differently to develop a more truthful and productive relationship with his manager.

Nobody likes to be criticized.

When the complaint is coming from a client directly or through a third-party interview, however, criticisms can actually be your best friend. Whether they're about you, your company, or your product, constructive criticism can provide a powerful opportunity for you to improve your sales technique, close more deals—and increase your revenues.

The key is to not respond defensively or angrily. Most salespeople—like most people period—get their dander up the moment anyone says anything even remotely negative. They get defensive, angry or, in the worst-case scenario, they look for ways to retaliate either overtly or covertly.

The following four-step process can help you learn how to take criticism well, and even begin to use it to enhance your client relationships.

Step 1. *Thank the client (or your manager) for their feedback.* Try saying something like "thanks for bringing this to my attention. I appreciate the opportunity you've given me to improve (the level of service, my responsiveness, and so on)."

Step 2. *Ask questions.* People love to teach others what to do. So involve your client in the solution by asking what suggestions he has that might help you improve. Asking questions will allow you and your client to have a constructive dialogue around the issue at hand. Who knows, the client may even make a suggestion you never thought of!

Step 3. *Listen.* Your client is entitled to his opinion. So whatever he has to say—hear him out.

Listen to what is being said, process it, reflect on it, and then use it to improve. Try taking notes to show that what is being said is important to you. If your client feels you're taking his opinion seriously, he'll be less likely to get angry and more willing to work with you to reach a resolution.

If you listen with the intent to improve, you'll have an even better chance of understanding your client's point of view. Use the listening techniques you've developed as a sales professional to ask probing questions or ask for examples. And remember: Let the client do at least 70 percent of the talking.

At the end of the conversation, summarize what the client has said to show that you understand. Then ask for one more opinion: what he thinks you should do to improve.

Step 4. *Commit to improve.* Finally, always let the client know that you appreciate his opinions and suggestions—and that you will be taking concrete steps to improve. You can even go so far as to ask whether the client would like you to check in with him again in a couple of weeks.

In the meantime, don't turn your back on what the client has said or try to forget about it. Spend some time looking for any validity in the criticism, and perhaps share the feedback with someone you can trust to tell you the truth. This will also give you a chance to look at the criticism from a neutral perspective. We know this can be hard to do, especially when it's coming from someone you like (or someone who signs your paychecks!).

Only you can give other people permission to make you feel bad. Interpreting criticism as a subjective opinion with a solution instead of a personal rebuke will help you grow, build better relationships and, ultimately, become more successful. So take the opinions and criticism of others personally! Use what they say to create an action plan to upgrade your performance, both personally and professionally.

Getting to the Truth

By realizing how much we train and condition people in sales and business—and by taking ownership of our assumptions— we can regain control of difficult situations. It puts an end to

the "blame game." When we don't blame someone, that person will be less likely to become defensive, and more recep-
tive to what we have to say.

Try the following in your conversations with clients: Instead
of saying, *"You make me think that . . . ,"* try saying, *"I am thinking . . . "* or even *"I find myself thinking this."* There are plenty
of ways to convey ownership; just do it in a style that feels right.

Let's apply that skill to everyday situations that we face as
salespeople. Here are two examples:

*"I noticed that you didn't have any questions during the presen-
tation. I have been wondering if you're unhappy with the solution?
What are your thoughts?"*

*"I noticed that you told me the proposal was okay. I'm thinking
that you're not really that pleased with it. Do you have any feedback to give me about it?"*

And if that doesn't work, here's how to confront a prospect
who may be lying.

Turn yourself into your favorite TV detective. Ours is
Horatio Crane from *CSI: Miami*. If Horatio Crane thought he
was hearing a conflicting or inconsistent story, he would rub his
head and say: *"Bob, I notice you said this, and now you are saying
that . . . I'm confused,"* or *"Could you clarify this?"* Smart strategy! By taking responsibility for his confusion, Horatio disarms
people and makes them feel comfortable enough to tell him the
things he needs to know to solve the problem.

When you think a prospect may be keeping the truth from
you, remember Horatio Crane. Stick to the facts, approach a
situation from the position that you are confused or unclear,
give your prospect the benefit of the doubt, and ask questions
sincerely to gain clarification. Here are some examples:

- *"Yesterday you mentioned that you were looking for a product
  that would do X, Y, and Z, and today you mentioned that*

getting the lowest price is the only consideration for your purchase. Did something change?"

- *"When you say you need a discount, how much do you need?"*
- *"When you say you need it next week, does that mean it has to be installed next week or just that it has to arrive on your premises to be ready for installation?"*
- *"I'm confused. Could you help me understand your new purchasing process?"*
- *"When you say we are too expensive, what do you mean by that?"*
- *"I notice that you are hesitating over my proposal. Maybe I missed something that was important to you. What are your thoughts about this?"*

Regardless of the point you wish to clarify, the CSI detective method will help you get to the bottom of an issue quickly. Remember, much of what makes this approach work—what makes it work for Horatio Crane—is that you have to genuinely want to find the answers and demonstrate that it may well be your fault for not understanding. Only with this attitude of responsibility will your questions be perceived as sincere. If you are asking these questions as a technique to trick your prospect or client into telling the truth—to catch them in a lie—your tonality will be interpreted as patronizing and disrespectful.

The Law of Reciprocity

What you give out, you will get back. In other words, we will receive from clients the same treatment that we give our clients. It's this law of reciprocity that is the key behind training people that what you say is what you mean. Every time. Think of this law as good karma, rooted in the philosophy of what goes around comes around, a fundamental tenet of persuasion and sales. In a selling relationship, clients prefer to give back to those who have first given to them. The more on time we are, the more on time they will be. The more honest we are, the more likely it is that others will be honest with us.

Anyone who has ever waited on tables in a restaurant knows this: Servers tend to get bigger tips by including some candies with the patron's bill. And psychology studies routinely show that the more candy servers leave, the bigger the tips they tend to receive.

That's the power of the Law of Reciprocity. It applies to all lines of work, including that of sales professionals. When we take responsibility for our actions, others tend to take responsibility for theirs. When others apologize, we tend to apologize in turn. Let's look at a common sales example. A client has missed a scheduled phone call.

We suggest you take responsibility and admit that it might have been your mistake (maybe you were wrong after all). Try a voice mail like this: *"Hi John this is Colleen from ACME, calling because I thought we had a call scheduled today at 3. Sorry I missed you and I hope I didn't get the date or time wrong. I should have confirmed by e-mail earlier this week. You can reach me at 111-1111, and I will try you again tomorrow at 2."*

Let's say your client does not take responsibility for missing this call and says, "Yeah, you should have e-mailed me." Then you could say: *"Are you saying that next time you would like me to remind you of our calls so we don't miss each other?"* If he agrees, he has just consented to an action plan that is in your control. If, on the other hand, he disagrees, you can follow up with: *"What do we need to do so that we can ensure these follow-up meetings happen as scheduled?"*

If you are struggling with clients being late for appointments, missing calls and deadlines, examine your own behavior as Alan did. Once he realized that his clients were late because he had been late previously, he changed his behavior and was always on time. As a result, his clients showed up on time for meetings, and stopped missing deadlines.

Summing Up with One Last Thought: Focus on What Matters

Do you have a client who is unhappy, despite all efforts you've made to satisfy him? Nothing works 100 percent of the time—including the Law of Reciprocity. Some difficult clients—about 10 percent, in fact—will remain that way no matter how much positive feedback you give them. It's not worth worrying about. These are clients you will never be able to satisfy. Concentrate on the other 90 percent of people who seek a profitable, balanced relationship with you.

Referral Selling: Ensuring Honest Relationships from the Start

W hen we were interviewing top sales performers for this book we asked clients to give examples of situations where they had been lied to by salespeople in the interview process or as vendors to their business. One client, Kevin, surprised us because he struggled to think of an example (sadly, everyone else we interviewed overflowed with examples). Kevin went on to explain that he worked by referral only. He hired only those candidates that were referred to him and bought and sold products only to people who were referred to him. As a result, trust was high in his selling relationships and honesty and openness commonplace. We got to thinking: Could there be something to this? Could you actually create an honest sales environment by selling to and buying from only people who were referred to you?

Yes you can.

Referrals are the best source of sales leads, closing up to 15 times faster than a cold lead because they arrive on your desk with trust present between both parties. Referrals are the most powerful tool in any salesperson's arsenal. A referred prospect is much more likely to be ready to listen to you, trust what you say and—ultimately—to buy from you. Referrals make your job easier and help you sell more with less effort and in less time. What else could any salesperson ask for?

So how can you get more referrals and ensure honesty in all your selling relationships?

Let's first ask, what have you done to deserve more referrals?

If you want to increase your referral rate, you have to start by asking yourself a number of questions about how you conduct business on a daily basis. The most important question is again: "How likable and trustworthy are you?"

Like everything else in sales, there is no magic "likability" bullet that works to build trust every time with every client to gain more referrals. However, the following are 13 of the best ways we've found to help you increase your referrals by putting the other person first—and simply having fun!

Be Honest and Obvious

Tell the client you will be asking for referrals. Don't trick them or be coy and subtle. When a client raves about your service or you, say: *"and of course now I am going to ask you for referrals!"* We find that when you do, everyone laughs, which causes relaxation and a dialogue focused on the types of new prospects you want to meet. Don't hide the fact that you want to be introduced to others like your most successful client. Be truthful about it.

Start a Monthly Advocate Program

Once a year, do a client genealogy to see who or what was responsible for all the additions to your client base. Odds are, you'll find between 5 and 20 primary referral sources, ranging from current clients to friends, partners, and suppliers.

Make an "advocate list" of these active referral sources, and develop a concrete plan to keep in touch with them on a regular basis. Every four to six weeks, for example, send them something of value—not a brochure or a promotional piece, but something they will actually value and use, like an article or book you think they will enjoy, a phone call, an invitation to lunch or breakfast, or even a referral for their business.

We can't stress this enough—whatever you send has to be of value to them, not simply an advertisement for you. After all, the goal is for you to help them improve their business, not your own. Think about it this way—what could you give them that will help grow their revenue? If you help to grow their business, trust us, it won't take long before they return the favor and help grow yours. For examples of what to send to your best referral sources, please visit www.honestysells.com to download a complimentary copy of our Advocate Worksheet.

Develop a Culture of Referrals

Another approach that can help you develop a steady stream of referrals is to ask questions that benefit your client first. One of our clients doubled her referrals simply by asking the following client-focused question at the end of every client meeting:

"Now . . . how can I help you?"

By putting the needs of her client first, she demonstrates that she truly cares about them. When people sense that you care, they tend to want to return the favor. In fact, you may find that many of your clients are genuinely surprised by a question like this, because no salesperson has ever asked them that before. And that's why your follow-up question is equally indispensable:

"You've helped my business grow by becoming part of our family network. I'd like to help your business grow, too. So let me ask you—what type of people do you want to meet to help increase your revenue?"

While We Are on the Subject of Giving . . .

Be willing to give referrals to your clients and suppliers. Try asking *"Steven, you sound like you do great work for your clients.*

Maybe I can help. Who is a good prospect for your business, and how would you like me to introduce them to you?"

Remind Your Clients of How You Will Contact Them

Try something like: *"Steven, quite often my clients like to recommend the work I do to others. In case you plan to do so, I thought you would like to know how I handle your referral. First, I always check to make sure it's okay that I use your name as the introduction, ask whether your contact knows I will be contacting him, and find out from you what the best way to contact your friend is. Only after this conversation with you will I make a call or send an e-mail based on your recommendation. I find that everyone is most comfortable when they know I'll be contacting them and have a sense of why."*

Write Some Letters

If you don't feel comfortable asking for referrals face-to-face, try the approach that's worked for salespeople, direct marketers, and hopeless romantics for centuries: Write a letter!

Regardless of the business you're in, an effective letter writing campaign can bring in a steady stream of new leads that will have an immediate and dramatic impact on your bottom line. When drafting your letter, the key is to make sure it says four things:

1. Thank them for their business.
2. Remind them how you met—especially if it was through a referral.
3. Ask them to send you some names.

4. Tell them that you will reward them with lunch or a gift basket if their referral turns into business.

Sound simple? That's because it is! And the real beauty is—it works! Since implementing this system one of our clients is receiving a steady stream of referrals everyday. Currently, she reports being "30 for 30," that is 30 referrals for 30 days.

And the record (should you try to beat it) stands at these statistics: 21 referrals, 18 meetings, and 9 sales!

All from one letter sent to one client! Here is our challenge to you: If you send this letter and get a better result than those stats above, we will reward you. Visit www.honestysells.com for full details of this exciting referral contest and your chance to win a great prize!

We'll even give you the tools. See Exhibit 9-1 for an example of how this letter looks. You are welcome to "steal" and adapt it for your own market. Why not try? It works.

Send Thank-You Notes and Gifts

Send a thank-you note for every referral and a gift for every referral that turns into business.

Thank-you notes should be handwritten, on a note card or postcard that isn't branded with your company advertising. Keep a supply of traditional, fun, themed, and plain note cards handy for all occasions throughout the year. For a real treat, spoil yourself with a great fountain pen to make writing the notes something you really look forward to.

One salesperson we know sends $50 to $100 gas station gift cards with a note to everyone who has referred business to his company. He includes a note reading: "Thanks! You filled up my tank, now it's my turn to fill up yours."

Exhibit 9.1   Who Says There is no Such Thing as a Free Lunch?

Dear _____,

I am writing to ask you a favor. As you can imagine, the best way for me to grow my business is by word of mouth. In fact, you and I were originally introduced by (Bob's) referral. In view of our productive partnership and the results we've achieved, I wonder if you might provide some names for me?

Are there three to four colleagues, acquaintances and/or friends inside or outside your organization to whom you can recommend me knowing that they would benefit from the kind of value you've seen me deliver? I greatly appreciate any suggestions you may have and I'd be willing to use your name or not as you see fit.

I want to reward you for referrals, so when you send us a prospect who becomes a client, we will send you (free lunch for two at XYZ local restaurant or a free gourmet gift basket for the office to enjoy at lunch).

I'll follow up with you (Date and Time) to see if this is acceptable and to see who you have come up with. Thanks in advance for your assistance. You know that I will also readily reciprocate in every way possible.

If it's easier, you can simply fill in the form below with your referral(s) and their contact information, and forward along to me by fax 111-111-1111 or in the mail with the enclosed envelope.

Best regards,
Colleen

Name	Company/Position	Phone	E-mail Address
1.		(. . .)	
2.		(. . .)	
3		(. . .)	
4.		(. . .)	
5.		(. . .)	

On the other hand, you don't have to send the same thing to everyone. Instead, take a minute to think about what your client would really like. If she's a dedicated oenophile, send wine. If he's into sports, try tickets to a game. For gourmets or candy-o-holics (like us), food baskets work wonders and are available in almost any size, style, and budget at the click of a mouse. Some of our favorite online gift sites are:

- www.harryanddavid.com
- www.elenis.com
- www.omahasteaks.com
- www.pattycakes.com
- www.candybouquet.com
- www.tiffany.com
- www.baskits.com
- www.montblanc.com
- www.ediblearrangements.com

Got some favorite sites of your own? We're always on the lookout for new ideas (not to mention new sources of gourmet delectables!). Visit the Honesty sells blog at www.honesty sells.com/blog to add to the list of gift sites all salespeople should use.

One last thing—we implore you *never* to send electronic greeting cards, no matter the occasion. E-cards look like you were too lazy or didn't care enough to do the real leg work needed to honor your client—and let's face it, that's not too far off the mark, is it?

Go the extra mile and write a personalized note. That little extra effort is what will get you noticed—and get you more referrals.

Bring Like-Minded People Together

Create a top-of-the-class networking club. Make a list of those people in your area who you know to be well-connected, great networkers, then invite them all to come together—with one catch: they have to bring someone that they think the rest of the group should meet. It's likely this person will be a great networker, too.

When great networkers get together in the same room, the energy is unmistakable, and they share leads like there's no tomorrow. Plus, because everyone in the room will be of the same caliber, there'll be an even higher propensity to share, because everyone will feel like the giving and receiving is balanced.

Pauline Fleming is an executive coach and friend of ours who uses this approach monthly to increase her network. She hosts a series of networking parties called "elbow rooms." Pauline invites like-minded Life Givers who are interested in connecting with people and sharing their contacts. The event is a permission-based referral party where everyone is free to ask for help and give help to others looking to obtain referrals for their businesses.

Honor Referrals

Every time you meet a new prospect through a referral, honor the person who made the referral. Talk about the person you know in common in a positive way and let your new prospect know how much you value the referring person. Share something that person taught you—of course without revealing something confidential or gossiping! In other words, show appreciation for your clients when you meet new prospects so they see firsthand that you operate from a position of integrity and generosity.

Have Fun with Holidays and Celebrations

Most salespeople send Christmas or holiday cards. But if you want to stand out and be remembered by your clients, why not try something a little different? In addition to sending cards out each December 25th, mix a few of the following ideas into your annual calendar:

- Valentine's Day candy baskets with the message "We love having you as a client."
- Birthday cakes on clients' birthdays.
- St Patrick's Day cards with a note about "being lucky to have them as a client."
- Champagne on the company's anniversary.
- Thank-you cards or gifts on the anniversary of their doing business with you.
- Gifts for their children's birthdays.
- Plants on the first day of spring or at Easter.
- Orange and black candy at Halloween.
- Gifts for your clients' administrative assistants on Secretaries' Day.
- Patriotic presents on national holidays (for example, Memorial Day, Victoria Day, or the Fourth—or First, in Canada—of July).
- Thanksgiving cards or food baskets.
- If your clients have volunteer days where they help out a local project in the community, see if you can participate with them.
- Send congratulations to your clients when you know they've completed something significant in their personal or

professional lives such as running their first 10K, earning a black belt in karate, or qualifying for the Boston Marathon.

See if you can top this:

*One client in Ohio uses Donut Day (the first Friday in June) to celebrate with his best clients and prospects. Every year he sends a thank-you card and a $5 Dunkin' Donuts*^{TM} *card to his 25 best prospects and 25 top clients. The card reads: "Happy Donut Day! Have a dozen on us." The response? The first year he tried it the campaign cost him $125 and returned more than $8,000 in sales. That is a return on investment of 6,300 percent! And, not surprising to us, he has repeated or beaten that number every year for the past three years.*

Donut Day may not be the holiday for you to celebrate but I bet there is a day that ties in nicely to your client base. Pick up a copy of *Chase's Calendar of Events*—or look at the plain old calendar on the wall—to take advantage of unique days that will make you stand out and be more referable to your clients.

Always Have Time

Sometimes our clients don't refer business to us because they see that we are busy serving them and others. They assume we have all the business that we need. If you are still growing and want new business make sure your clients don't make a wrong assumption! Simply say to your clients, "I'm never too busy to see if I can help your friends, family, or colleagues."

Be World Class!

After your product is delivered or your service is complete say to your clients "One of the ways I know I'm doing a good job for my clients is when they tell others about me. I know that only happens when you think I am providing world class service to you. My goal is that at some point, you will trust me enough to consider me as someone you can trust to help other people you know. Sound okay?"

Ask

How Not to Ask for Referrals

When talking to others, unless you're specific in your questions, you risk getting an unfavorable response. Here are some examples of questions that are simply too vague:

- Who else do you know that might benefit from our services?
- Do you know anyone else I should talk to?

How to Ask for Referrals

You can expect a favorable response from specific requests such as:

- I'm trying to meet . . . of . . . BAC Corp. Do you know him?
- Do you have other branch or field offices that manage IT services as well?
- Do you have an IT director in your New York Office?
- Do you have a marketing department that runs special events?

Summing Up

At its most basic level, selling is relationship building. And to build a successful relationship, you have to know a few things about the other person who's in the relationship with you. Yes, some of these ideas require you to know detailed information about your clients. But isn't that what sales is all about?

There are countless ways you can let your clients know you care and are thinking about them. Each has its pros and cons. Some work consistently but are expensive. Others are cheap and easy to implement, but don't produce as many leads as you might want. Try them all, and try them often, and we'll guarantee, you'll start to see results—and more referrals—in no time.

Asking for referrals can be a double-edged sword. On the one hand it's important that you're not obnoxious about asking for referrals nor that you look like you are begging. Nobody trusts a desperate-looking or -sounding sales rep! On the other hand, you must be persistent and consistent and find subtle ways to remind your clients that you are always open to receiving referrals and new prospects. Creating a referral strategy based on the 13 principles outlined in this chapter will help you find the right balance. You'll never hurt a relationship; you'll build openness and virtually ensure honesty in all your sales relationships.

The Start of Your Selling Relationship: Getting Started with an Honest Foot Forward

The fastest way to get what you want is first to help others get what they want.

—Yogi Berra

W hen we walk into our prospective clients' offices, call them on the phone, or send them an e-mail for the first time, the first question they ask themselves is likely: "What's the point of this? What's in it for me?"

Understanding helps the prospective clients understand why we are addressing them in the first place. Clarifying our purpose puts everyone at ease. Have you ever been in a sales call where the prospect has lost sight of the purpose for the encounter? When prospective clients do not understand what our purpose or intention is, they get nervous; they wonder (sometimes out loud), "Why are you asking me these questions?" Next, they become defensive, guarded, and less likely to share information with you.

Commonality of purpose unites you with the people with whom you work on a given project. It builds a rapport that leads to trust and to the development of a long-term, profitable relationship. This is because the purpose—what you want out of a sales interaction—should be what the other person wants; and if they are in alignment with your purpose, they will be more likely to help you find a solution.

It is essential that our communication has direction and purpose. When we have a clear idea of a desired outcome, our sales conversations and presentations are focused on that goal.

The best behavioral change that we can make as sales professionals is to simply get over ourselves and start focusing on our clients and prospects. They are not interested in what we have to say unless they can see how it is in their best interests. Sales guru Zig Ziglar once said that the most popular radio station in the world is WII FM, which is short for: "What's In It For Me?"

It is remarkable how many times we have encountered salespeople who complain about not making a sale by saying: *"I knew exactly what the client needed. It was so obvious to me, but I lost the sale. How could the prospect have been so blind?"* The mistake here is that salespeople often focus on themselves rather than on what the client wants to buy. We cannot be persuasive if our focus is on us. An easy way to reframe your approach to ensure that your client's interests are always at the forefront is to answer three questions:

1. Who cares? Who are you selling to? Be as specific as possible. Is it to all the marketing VPs in the textile industry? Is it to mothers of newborn babies? Or is it to all the chief technology officers in the aerospace industry?

2. Why us? In other words, what made your past clients pick your company, product, or service? The answer to this question is what defines your product. For example, it might be your tradeshow booth, your retirement-planning system, your clothing line, or your human resource staffing services.

3. So what? This is where you answer the question "What's in it for them?" What's the benefit of them buying the "why us?"

Put your answers to these questions together, and you'll get a statement that may sound something like this:

"You mentioned that you are working with a very restricted budget. The VPs of marketing at banks across Canada and the United States are buying our tradeshow equipment because it can cut by up to 40 percent the labor and shipping costs while still

maintaining durability. Knowing that, does it make sense for you to look at our product line?''

You might want to take a cue from the world's best persuaders: children. Children realize quickly that in order to get what they want they must convince others—the people of whom they are asking a favor—how they will benefit. Notice how children will say: "Buy me this, and I will love you more," "Take me to this place, and I will clean up my room," and, of course, our favorite: "Let me do this and I'll stop bugging you."

How can we be sure that our product or service features are presented with our clients' interests as the focus? The answer is to refocus our presentation of these features to highlight the benefit to the client. We must remain aware of the six core motivators that drive human behavior—which can be described as emotional triggers.

Using emotional triggers is not about manipulating another person; rather, it is about respecting the individual and responding in a manner that will meet that person's needs. Rather than complaining because someone is not cooperating with us, think about what solutions you are providing and reframe them to highlight what's in it for your client. And if you are not sure how to answer that question—then you can always ask.

It's true that this effective sales strategy—"Focus on the client"—may appear to be obvious and overly simplistic. It's our experience, however, that common sense does not equal common practice.

Rather than stating "I know this already," ask yourself, "When is the last time I put this into practice?"

When was the last time that a client requested information from you, and you proceeded to sell based on what you thought the best product features were—rather than letting the client buy what he really wanted?

Remember this universal truth: Focusing on the client is the key to getting what you want. Here are the emotional triggers you can use to focus your message squarely on your clients.

Greed

As Zig Ziglar once said, "*Money isn't everything, but it ranks right up there with oxygen.*" It represents the means by which we attain any material or service, from our basic necessities to the luxuries we afford ourselves.

How does what you are selling make your clients more money or help them save more profit?

Time

It's staggering how many people are time-impoverished; almost everyone wishes that there were more hours in the day.

How does what you're selling save your clients time or make their jobs easier? Can your product make your clients more effective and efficient? How?

Fear

People tend to avoid risk in search of security. One example of fear-based decision making was the old saying, "Nobody gets fired for buying IBM." Back in the late 1990s, many high tech companies tried to capitalize on a "FUD" (Fear, Uncertainty, and Doubt) selling strategy to sell high-priced computer systems and services knowing that many people were afraid the turn of the century could wreck havoc on their computers' internal systems.

Does what you sell help anyone resolve a specific fear? If you sell services that help with government compliance issues you could say that you help alleviate the fear of noncompliance or crackdowns.

Gain

All of us enjoy producing results. If your solution will help a prospect accomplish something he needs to achieve, you will grab his attention. For example, if your request will help your client achieve his sales target, then you will be more likely to attract his attention.

How can you make your clients look good? Can your products help them get a promotion? A raise? Can you make them look like heroes?

Guilt

Does not having your product make the client feel inferior in any way? Is there peer pressure or social pressure that can be used to make a client want what you have? Will your clients be considered to be behind the times if they don't buy from you? Guilt drives people to make decisions that will improve the lives of others, especially where their families are concerned.

Can you show that people who have not bought your product have been left behind or overlooked?

Contribution

People will work hard if they feel like they could really make a difference. Look what is happening in our country today. People will often help out if they feel like what they are asked to do will really make a difference.

How can your product or service help to make a difference? Do charities or nonprofits buy your product? Are your clients contributing to global conservation projects? If a company buys your product will it be contributing to a bigger picture or solution in some way?

Pride

We are all concerned about what others think. We often just lie about it and say, *"I don't care what they think,"* when usually, we really do. The power of image and reputation is why so many of us have a hard time saying "no." So if your solution affects people's image or reputation, then you will likely capture their attention.

Does your product make people stand out? Is it likely that if they buy from you others will take notice and give your client applause?

Love

People will go to great lengths to have more enjoyment in their lives. If you are not enjoying your current situation with a client or a colleague, realize they are probably not enjoying it either. Discover and communicate "what's in it for them."

What can you offer that will bring joy and happiness to your client? What do your clients find happiness in?

Summing Up

Success in business is about helping your clients—not helping yourself!

Top performers put their clients first, because they know that they'll never succeed at an elite level if their objective is solely to sell stuff to other people. The top 10 percent know that they can only be successful if they're focused instead on helping other people to buy. For most salespeople, this represents a fundamental shift in their mindset. How do you begin this transition? By focusing on the client and addressing the "what's in it for me" factor.

Top salespeople never try to sell a product to a client without first knowing whether they can help. In fact, top performers will gladly walk away from a prospect if they don't think the product or service they have to offer will be of use. Remember: honest selling isn't about telling a prospect what you think they want to hear. Honest selling is about starting a dialogue to uncover a prospect's problem and then helping them solve that problem in the best way possible.

Close More Sales by Acknowledging Your Clients

If we would just support each other, that's 90 percent of the problem.

—Edward Gardner

S o far, we have addressed a number of techniques in this book that will make a difference in the way you sell. They will produce results. Successful salespeople—the top-ranked ones in any organization—go out of their way to build deep rapport, and high trust relationships with their prospects and clients. They demonstrate that they genuinely care about people, feel empathy or compassion for their problems, and sincerely want to help them. Honest salespeople don't "pitch" prospects or sell features and benefits. They don't pressure with limited-time offers and discounts. Most important, they don't talk as much as they listen. They pay attention to their clients first and themselves second.

They appreciate their clients and the business that is transacted, and they are grateful for the relationship personally and professionally. Top performing salespeople understand that closing a sale is not about them—it's about the client. They focus on creating a positive client experience that is based on trust, appreciation, and honesty. As a result, few—if any—of their clients look elsewhere when they need to re-order. In terms of percentages, the salesperson who builds deeper rapport and remembers to acknowledge her clients can expect to do 70 to 80 percent of her business each year with her existing client base.

The Key to Acknowledgment

A powerful driving force in all human beings as noted in the emotional triggers of selling in Chapter 10 is the desire to make a difference. We want to see that our lives count, and we need to feel that we matter to someone; that we are noticed and important. That's why acknowledgment is important. To acknowledge a client is to say: I see you, I appreciate your business. You are significant to me.

It's simple to show acknowledgment. Just remember that the key when it comes to the art of acknowledging people, is get in GEAR!

G: *Genuine.* Say it only if you mean it. People know when you are being insincere.

E: *Exact.* Explain what you are acknowledging exactly. Don't just say, *"Thanks for doing a good job."* Say: *"I appreciate the work you did on the Jones project. Your attention to detail on the contract negotiation was outstanding!"*

A: *At once.* Catch people doing something good and acknowledge it right away. Don't wait a week. Do it now. Even if you have to make a phone call or send an e-mail rather than acknowledging someone in person. An immediate acknowledgment is always better than a delayed one.

R: *Regular.* You cannot harm people by overappreciating them.

Who Doesn't Need to Hear These Things?

Sales professionals ask us if it is possible to overacknowledge. We tell them no! Not if the acknowledgment is genuine. You should never be concerned with quantity of this recognition but rather the quality of the gesture. Is the acknowledgment truly sincere? To our knowledge, no one has ever left an organization or refused to buy a product because they were acknowledged or supported too much. Remember the statistic from Chapter 6: 67 percent of lost business each year is lost because of clients who imagine that you are indifferent to their needs and wants. Have you, as a consumer ever stopped doing business with a company because you perceived that the staff didn't care?

Acknowledgment requires more than singling someone out and showering them with praise or gifts. There are also implicit support behaviors in recognizing another person's efforts and work—and these should be worked into your daily sales calls and routines for all interactions.

Be Empathetic and Compassionate

Truly care about your client (no matter how good an actor you are, faking it won't work). Ask questions, take notes, and lean in to show that you're engaged in the client's answers. When you take an interest in people, they remember you— and when people remember you, it's good for business.

Observe the other person's eyes, handshake, body language and tone of voice.

Try to capture the physical impression your prospect makes, then try to match it.

Make Eye Contact

This is especially important when you walk into a room full of people. It's also essential after we get to know people, because it cements our existing relationships and lets them know that we're still interested in their well-being. Very few salespeople ever look their prospects directly in the eye. You'll be surprised how much simply smiling and making eye contact will set you apart from other salespeople.

Give Value First

Share your network of contacts with your clients, and don't expect them to give you their business without you giving them something first. Look to offer things that will increase your value. Perhaps a client needs a referral to a partner of yours or requires some help finding a new dentist. Or maybe a prospect has a business problem that can be fixed with a new idea you read about or heard from someone else you've met. Can you offer a subscription to a magazine full of articles to help your prospect at her job? Does your company have a high-value newsletter or white paper that you can distribute?

Express Your True Intent

Tell clients upfront: *"I don't know if there's a fit between what you need and what I have right now, but I'm hoping we can explore that in more detail during this meeting."* Or try this: *"I only have your best interests at heart, and I promise to be honest with you throughout our conversation. In the end, I hope that we can mutually decide if there is a reason to move forward. If not, that's fine, too, and I hope you'll feel comfortable telling me so."* The thought of speaking to someone like that might make you uncomfortable, because it runs counter to the business habits that we witness every day. But that's one of the reasons why only 10 percent of salespeople in any organization are top performers; they do things that most others don't. Try expressing your true intent. Say it to yourself a few times. You'll be amazed at the response you get.

Don't Go for the Big Decision All at Once

We would never consider proposing marriage to someone with whom we've never been on a date, would we? Well, the same is true for our business relationships. You must obtain approval from your client to move ahead in increasing increments. All too often, salespeople jump way ahead of their prospect's buying curve, which puts the buyer and the seller out of sync. If you are trying to close while the prospect is still evaluating options or determining risk, trust is broken and the prospect feels pushed—and the sale comes dangerously close to disappearing.

Use Friendly, Warm Words Instead of Formal Business Speak

When you use simple language, people respond better and trust you more. So limit your words to three syllables or fewer. Don't try to impress prospects with your extensive vocabulary—you run the risk of sounding inauthentic. It's true that there are some words in English that are more influential than others. Check out the words that build trust below:

You

Need

Discover

Easy

Results

Proven

Health

Love

Money

Save

Safe

Guarantee

New

Help

Why?

Did you notice that all the words are simple, plain, friendly words that everyone can use every day? It's no surprise. You build the deepest trust and are the most influential with clients when you speak a language that your clients understand. Warning: Putting all the words together in one sentence does not make the world's most influential sentence! Be authentic with your language; pick and choose the right words for the right situation.

Use People's Names . . . with Care

When it comes to using names, there are just two rules to follow: Be aware of whether someone is comfortable being addressed on a first-name basis or not, and never overuse a person's name; doing so only sounds corny and false. Dale Carnegie once said, "*Nothing is so beautiful to a person as the sound of their own name.*" Just use your discretion.

Thank You. Thank You Very Much

Thank-you cards are a simple, inexpensive way to show clients appreciation. They can be tied directly to receiving more business and referrals. Clients who feel appreciated buy more and buy more often. A simple way to use them is to write a thank-you card at the time an order is placed, when a client reorders, and at the anniversary date of when someone became a client. When was the last time you received a thank-you card from a vendor?

A top 10 percent best practices tip: Choose your thank-you cards to match the personality of your client. If you know they love dogs, send thank-you cards with dogs on them. Send cat cards to your cat-loving clients and food cards to your foodies (Colleen even keeps a stack of Elvis cards for her Elvis fan clients). Don't know what your client will prefer? Simply send a plain card on exceptional stationery. No logos. No corporate messages. This is the time for a personal outreach, not a corporate one.

When you send a card with the client's interest on the front, she may keep that card on her desk for weeks or months. And, every time she sees it, she thinks of you. When others come into the office and see the card they ask about it. And guess what? You are mentioned again. With that one little card you can stay top of mind and are more likely to be thought of first when add-on business is required or referrals are available.

Summing Up

Your success will ultimately be directly determined by your willingness to acknowledge your client base and your ability to network. In good times or bad, the type of salesperson you choose to be is entirely up to you. Choose to be kind, honest, open, and supportive of your clients. You'll see consistent sales growth; you'll build an excellent reputation; and you'll become a leader in your field—regardless of your market or the state of the economy.

The Honest Way to Close More Sales. More Often. More Quickly.

To ask the right question is already half the solution to the problem.

—Carl Jung

O pen communication is at the root of successfully closing sales. So far, we have talked about the steps that
you can take to build an honest communication environment between you and your clients, but how do you use it
to bring in more business? By fine-tuning your sales questioning skills to be more effective and getting a dialogue started
and keeping it flowing.

In sales, there's a fine line between simply being inquisitive
and getting to know your client and conducting an interroga-
tion. The consequences of stepping over this line could cost
you the sale, lose you business or—worse yet—lose you a loyal
client for life.

The key to staying on the right side of this line lies in the
questions you ask, and especially *how* you ask them. The following questioning tips will help you make sure you're perceived as being helpfully inquisitive rather than an
uncompromising interrogator, and they will help you improve
your delivery when it comes to asking those all-important
sales questions.

Making Sure You Don't Cross the Line

Have you ever been in a conversation with someone who just
drones on and on about their opinions without once stopping
to listen to what you might have to say? We don't know about
you, but whenever we find ourselves trapped in a conversation
with one of these people, it takes every ounce of our self-
restraint not to scream, "Who cares?!" In fact, we have yet to

meet a client who enjoys the experience of having a salesperson force opinions and perceptions on him—even (or perhaps especially) when that salesperson felt she was only offering her honest opinion.

The mistake most salespeople make is thinking that it is our opinions and perceptions that influence the client to buy. The fact is, most successful salespeople find that the complete opposite is true: They are far more successful when they don't express their perceptions but instead limit their communication entirely to the facts and their experiences.

It is our job as salespeople to listen to the opinions of the client and tailor solutions to fit those opinions—not to force our opinions on others.

Staying on the Right Side of the Fine Line

Successfully staying on the right side of this line depends entirely on your ability to get your clients to share with you their emotional reasons for buying your products. How do you do this? You must ask them the right questions—questions that will move your prospects from an intellectual position (knowing they have a problem that needs to be solved) to the emotional state of trusting you to solve that problem in a way that will satisfy them.

The right questions, in other words, are ones that will help you to reveal a buyer's true motivations. To help you get the answers to those questions—and close more deals in the process—try the following four steps to build lasting and profitable client relationships:

1. Identify the current situation or problem.

- What's the biggest challenge that you are facing today in your area?

- Our clients tell us that we help them solve problems in the area of X. Is that a problem area for you?
- Our other clients in this industry have discovered that we can help solve X, Y, and Z problems with their production line. Which is the most important to you?
- What problem matters most to your business?

2. Get acquainted with the details.

- Can you tell me more about your problem?
- Could you be more specific?
- How long have you had this concern?
- What have you done to address it?
- How did that work out?
- How do you mean?
- What if you do nothing?
- What makes you think . . . ?
- How have you employed solution X, Y, or Z?
- What has been your experience with solution X, Y, or Z?
- If you could change one thing, what would it be?

3. Identify the specific business impact of a problem.

- How has this problem impacted on your organization?
- If you had to guess, how much do you think this problem is costing your department?
- What will happen if this problem continues?
- How will your toughest competitor react to that?
- How much is one new client worth?
- How much is one new business friend or relationship worth?

4. Identify the specific personal impact of this problem.

- What impact does this problem have on your job or on your staff?
- How important is this to you personally?
- Why is it so important?
- What will happen if you don't find a solution to this problem?
- If you were able to achieve your goals, would it be worth it?
- Is that what you really want?
- How will you use that to your advantage?
- How will you deal with that?
- What plans have you made to handle that?

Remember: as salespeople, we're looking for information we can use to help our clients—not a confession. So why do so many sales professionals treat their prospects like criminal suspects rather than valuable business partners?

Here are five tips that will help you appear helpfully inquisitive.

1. Pause and listen.

Let's be honest—do you *really* listen to what your clients have to say, or are you just catching your breath between questions? If that sounds a little too familiar, try counting silently to three (at a regular speaking pace) every time your prospect finishes talking. This will give the other person enough time to gather his thoughts and continue speaking if he hasn't finished while not being awkwardly long if he has finished talking and is simply waiting for your response.

2. Support what they tell you only when you mean it. Before you ask your next question, make sure to thank your prospect for the information she has already provided in response to your previous one. It's not always easy for a prospect to open up, especially in the early stages of your relationship. If a prospect has been generous with information, thank her for being open. If she asks a great question, thank her for it. But while this approach can yield great results, don't ever fake a compliment or expression of gratitude. If you don't truly believe what you are telling and thanking your prospects for, then believe me, you won't be fooling anyone but yourself.

3. Take notes and ask for clarification. To make sure you remember the details as well as the substance of what clients tell you, take notes, and ask for clarification any time they say something you don't fully understand. Remember, in sales, your best friends are "why," "how," and "what." Use them often to get additional information from your clients—and then don't forget to document their answers!

4. Echo and paraphrase. They say that you never really understand something until you have to teach it to someone else. To be certain you really understand what clients tell you, repeat it back to them using your own words and interpretation. Then end with a question, to gain their confirmation that your understanding is correct.

5. Watch your tone! We never cease to be amazed at how many professional salespeople ask questions of even their biggest clients or most promising prospects in a tone that sounds aggressive, accusatory, or downright belligerent. If you've ever gotten the sense that you're coming on a little too strong, practice asking a colleague questions to determine whether you sound inquisitive or interrogational. If this isn't an option, take your manager with you on a call, and ask him for constructive, honest feedback. Ninety-three percent of the way prospects react to your questions will be based not on what you ask but on how you ask. Finding out how you really sound could make the difference between being an average performer and skyrocketing to the top of your profession.

Summing Up

If closing profitable business, building long-term relationships, and gaining lasting competitive advantage is what you hope to achieve in sales, then you need to develop honest selling techniques that don't leave you or your prospect feeling beaten up, manipulated or "hard done by" at the end of the selling process. Too many times we see salespeople who are willing to do and say almost anything to get the sale. The end result? A tenuous relationship between a client who never trusts, who thinks her salesperson doesn't understand what she really needs, and who feels she needs to constantly shop the solution to keep her sales rep honest; and a salesperson who resents his client for being too much work and for being ungrateful for the effort he expended on the client's behalf.

In short, nobody's happy.

How do we change the way we close business to ensure that we maintain strong, profitable, and lasting relationships? First, we need to make a fundamental shift in thinking around what we consider closing the sale to be about.

Closing business today is not about wrestling your prospect to the mat at the end of a long and confusing sales cycle. Today, closing depends on customizing a solution based on what the client really wants. What does your client want? The answer depends 100 percent on your ability to ask the right questions in the right way.

Overcoming Objections and Questions

S o now that we've talked about how you can ask questions honestly to create a winning sales dialogue we turn our attention to how you can answer questions honestly as well.

We believe that people—and your clients—want a "good listening to," not "a good talking to." Don't you agree?

The biggest hurdle that most salespeople have to overcome is to listen to the messages that we really don't want to hear. Questions and objections are a natural response from any serious buyer about to engage in a substantial investment. Despite the fact that hesitation is a normal part of the buyer's decision-making process, most salespeople don't recognize the real reason behind why it happens; and they react badly when it does. If all serious decision makers have questions before making a major purchase, isn't it likely that a prospect might hesitate as well?

More important, if hesitation and questions are a natural response from serious buyers, what is the best way to address them? The common approach for dealing with questions and objections is one that is fatal to the sales process: panic. You can avoid this mistake, however, by learning to understand the real meaning behind the client's objection. Remember that your prospect's hesitation is just a defense mechanism designed to protect him against the risk of making a wrong decision. Your job is to help your prospect discover that engaging with you is the right decision.

How Can We Control Our Surprise and Stop the Panic?

First, let's look at the best way to reduce the overall number of objections you are experiencing. Quite simply, the most effective way to reduce hesitation at the end of the selling cycle is to call high early (to executives) and to be proactive in addressing concerns. Bring questions or objections up first. As a preventative measure, if you run into a certain objection a lot, bring it up first. For example, if you know that your price is never the lowest, you might suggest this to your prospect early in the sales cycle.

"Bob, I appreciate all the information you have provided regarding your project, and based on what you have said, I think our products may be able to help you. However, I want to tell you up front that although we are not the most expensive option, we are not ever the cheapest. Knowing this, does it make sense for us to continue with this process?"

If your prospect is going to hesitate and raise questions about your product eventually, you are better to be proactive, bring them up early, and tackle the concerns head on so you can move through the sale with ease.

Now, let's assume you have done all the right things and you still have hesitation or objections at the end of the sales cycle—don't worry. It happens to even the top 10 percent of salespeople some of the time. What should you do?

It's important to understand the real meaning of objections. Prospect hesitation should come as no surprise if you think about it this way: Anyone, yourself included, who is about to make a large investment thinks twice about that decision before making a commitment. When prospects are seriously considering your product, it is natural for them to be nervous and reevaluate the criteria to make sure that they are not making the wrong decision. Real prospects, ones with decision-making power, almost always become critical at final decision-making stages. They are examining their own internal justifications and knocking the idea around vigorously to be sure it is not defective. But remember, prospects do this because they are seriously thinking about engaging. A large investment is at stake, and saying yes is risky.

Viewing objections as negative and ignoring them until the end of the selling process causes salespeople to panic and revert to aggressive nonconsultative selling tactics. We stop asking questions, stop caring about the client's concerns, and our confidence disappears. We talk too much, defend our position, and practically beg for the order— maybe we start discounting? The deal begins to evaporate as we launch an aggressive defense, fighting for our point of view, rather than working toward an understanding of our prospect's real issues.

Next time, try to avoid adversarial tactics and panic. Remember that your prospect's hesitation is just a defense mechanism designed to protect against the risk of making a wrong decision. Your job is to help your prospect discover that engaging with you is the right decision.

Improve Your Objection-Handling Attitude

- Preempt the prospect's objection. Bring it up first and deal with it together early on.
- Help the prospect discover the answer to the question. Be curious, ask questions, and find a way to lead the prospect to his own answer.
- Remember that hesitation is a natural part of the buying process. It's a sign that your prospect is seriously

interested in buying, not a sign that he is trying to end the deal.

Examine Your Behavior

Why are you panicking? Are you doing something to provoke this behavior in your prospects? Maybe you can prevent or reduce hesitation from occurring:

- Keep your sales funnel full of prospects so that losing one will not be a big deal.
- Record common hesitations and questions and look for trends and patterns.
- For reoccurring questions, prepare an effective response in advance. Practice these responses with someone outside your sales and marketing department. Try other clients, engineers or consultants.
- Use your new responses and track the results you are getting.

Appreciate Your Prospect's Hesitation and Try the Following

- Don't panic, and stay in control. To be in control requires that you are prepared. Practice and prepare optimal responses to the most common questions about your product, services, and company.
- Ask questions to truly understand your prospect's reality. Don't make statements, especially defensive ones.
- Acknowledge when a prospect's position is correct. For example, *"Bob, you are right, we are not the lowest priced product available on the market."*

- State that you understand your prospect's position, even if you don't necessarily agree. *"Bob, I can understand that you are not happy with the price; have you seen something lower in the market?"*

- To get at the truth, try making statements that are just a tad more negative than your prospect's. *"Does this mean it's over between us, Bob?"* or *"I guess price is the only deciding factor?"* Going negative in this instance will help build the momentum for your prospect to swing back to the positive.

- Question, question, and question again until you're sure you understand.

- Ask your prospect for suggestions on how the business could move forward.

- Reintroduce your prospect to his original problem—balance his problems against your offered solution.

- Be creative—ask you prospect up front, *"If I can't find a solution to this objection, does that mean that it is over between us?"*

A Specific Note about Pricing Objections and Negotiations

We didn't feel it was right to write a sales book without including information on how to deal with the "pricing objection" in an open honest way. It seems as though these days every sales training course we teach, every client we coach, and every company we consult with is looking for ways to address the issue. Here are the common challenges we hear from clients:

- *"Your prices are too high."*
- *"Why are you so expensive?"*
- *"I have another offer, so you're going to have to do better than that!"*

The dreaded pricing negotiation. We've all had to deal with it at some point in our careers. Regardless of what form it takes, it can be one of the most frustrating challenges sales professionals have to face. Let's start by tackling the question of how to prevent the pricing negotiation before your clients bring it up.

Deal with It—Up Front, Honestly

If price always seems to become an issue for you, one of the most honest and effective strategies is to preempt the question by dealing with it up front. Don't be afraid to talk about price. Train yourself to bring it up first and get it on the table as early as possible in the sales dialogue. Try telling your prospective client something like:

"You need to know that ours is not the cheapest product available. You will always find someone who is less expensive than us, and you will always find someone who is more expensive than us. We are always competitive. Knowing that we are not the cheapest, does it make sense for us to go ahead?"

When you ask this question, one of two things will happen:

1. The sales cycle will end right there, because the client only wants the cheapest product and you don't have it. This is good news, because there's no point wasting your valuable time with someone who has no intention of doing business with you anyway.

2. The client will say: *"No problem, we're not making our decision on the basis of price alone."* This will effectively eliminate the client's ability to raise this objection later on and allow you to move forward with a high degree of certainty that price will not become an issue.

Provide an Early Estimate

Another way to reduce the number of times you hear "your price is too high" is by telling your clients your price (or an estimate of your price) before you give it to them in writing. This will allow you to deal with any potential pricing concerns in person before your client receives a formal proposal.

Note: If you must estimate, be as accurate as possible. If you really are unsure, it's always better to go a bit higher to give yourself some breathing room and ensure the most accurate proposal. Never inflate your price arbitrarily for the intent of negotiating it back down to list price: This is a manipulative sales practice, not an honest one. Tell your customer that this price is your "best guess" and could be higher or lower in the final proposal based on what they specifically need. The estimate we give is always about 20 percent higher than we have seen in the past, just to make sure we have breathing room later if the client has additional customizations. Of course, if the price is lower than the estimate we gave, we always give the lower price. That is the *only* way to ensure honesty in this process!

Have Your Options Ready

When you're ready to negotiate price, have several options prepared beforehand to handle your client's response, whatever it may be. This will enable you to retain some control and momentum regardless of whether the reaction is positive or negative.

If the client reacts negatively through body language such as by flinching, shrugging, rolling their eyes or falling off the chair and onto the floor, you can ask:

"I sense that you're uncomfortable with that price. What were you expecting?"

Or:

"You don't seem happy with that price. Have you found something lower?"

Notice that both of these questions have two distinct parts. First, you acknowledge that the client appears to be uncomfortable. This will help build trust and get the client on your side by checking in with your assumptions. Next, you ask a direct question. You can use this formula every time you are faced with an objection.

If the client verbally tells you that your price is too high, your first move is to take a breath and remain quiet for a full three seconds. Then ask: *"I guess you're looking only for the cheapest price?"*

The client will either say yes or no. If he says no, you can ask: *"Really? What else is there?"* If he answers yes, you can say: *"Okay, knowing that we will not be the lowest price, does that mean we will never get the chance to do business together?"*

The Most Powerful Word for Handling Objections

When it comes to handling pricing objections, "never" is the most powerful word in the sales language.

Most people hate it. Very few are willing to commit to it. As a result, the vast majority of clients will respond to it by saying, *"well, no . . . not never!"*

In that case, your job is simply to ask: *"Really? Why?"* The client will then either tell you what it will take to do business with him or ask you for something that you can't provide. Either way, you get the real answer. This approach puts the control back in your hands by letting you choose between making the sale or turning down the deal and walking away.

If a client is dead set on getting the lowest price and you know you can't offer it, then you may as well end the conversation right there and get to work on deals that have a better likelihood of closing. Spending time trying to sell to someone who is never going to buy from you is both a bad decision—and a costly mistake.

Brainstorm Your Best Answers

Finally, take some time to sit down (on your own or with your team) and brainstorm your best possible answers to every potential objection. Practice your responses out loud until you've mastered them. Make them your own. Then review your work each quarter to make sure that everyone on your team knows which responses are working best.

If you can reduce the number of objections you receive, you will sell more. Period.

Hitting the Objection Head On!

Perhaps you were not successful at preventing the objection from happening and now you are faced with a client complaining about your prices. What to do? Here is a proven two-step formula that can help you handle any pricing (or any other) negotiation, for those times when your ounce of prevention may not be 100 percent foolproof.

Step 1: Count to Three

Whenever you're faced with a difficult question or objection, the first thing you need to do is take a deep breath, make eye contact with your prospect, and silently count to three.

It is amazing how many clients will answer their own objections, or at least give you some much-needed information, when you simply say nothing. Don't be afraid of silence. Practice it until the three-second pause becomes one of the most effective tools in your arsenal.

A couple of years ago, Colleen was buying a new pair of glasses and having lenses put in an old pair. The optician was clearly afraid to talk about price, and even went so far as to write the estimate down on a piece of paper and pass it to her instead of saying the price out loud.

To Colleen's surprise, the number actually struck her as very reasonable. She had left her purse at home, so she turned to her husband to get his wallet. The optician took Colleen's silence as an objection and immediately dropped the price 15 percent.

This seemingly minor transaction was a great demonstration of the power of silence, and the lengths most people will go to in order to fill it. In sales, you can use silence to effectively handle almost any objection, particularly those related to price.

Whenever a client tells you your price is too high, just breathe and be quiet. You will find that around 40 percent of all prospects will fill that silence with information you can use to move the sale forward.

Step 2: Ask Questions

You can ask up to three questions before you have to answer an objection—provided you ask the right questions in the right way. The key is to acknowledge what the client is saying and then offer a compliment or empathetic statement before asking your question. For example, try saying something like, *"I appreciate you asking that," "That's a really great question," "I understand how you feel,"* or *"Good point, I never thought about that!"*

Including a nice, warm statement in front of your question will encourage your client to answer it, because the client will feel like you are giving her something first. The compliment is a gift. It makes her feel that she is special, that you are paying attention to her and that you truly care about her, and she will be more likely to respond in kind.

Which Questions to Ask?
Once you've paid the client a compliment, ask him a question that is both direct and phrased to elicit more information. The following are some responses you can use to answer a few of the more common objections.

Objection: "Your Price Is Too High!"
Honest Negotiation Responses

- *Thanks for sharing that. How much too high are we?*
- *I appreciate your telling me that. Have you found a less expensive product?*
- *You are right; we are more expensive than some of our competitors. How much were you hoping to pay?*
- *You're right, we are not the cheapest. Is price the only consideration?*
- *Thanks for being honest. Is the price higher than you expected, or is it because we combined the services and training in one proposal?*
- *I'm not surprised to hear you say that. Are we only too high overall or is our per-unit cost too high as well?*

- *Thanks for sharing that. Is our price a showstopper?*
- *I appreciate your honesty. Does our current price mean we will never be able to do business together?*
- *Too high? Really?*
- *What do you suggest we do?*
- *Thanks for letting me know. I'm curious, how much were you expecting to invest?*

Objection: "We Don't Have Any Budget"
Honest Negotiation Responses

- *Budget?*
- *Oh! I appreciate that makes it difficult to buy. When does your budget come up for renewal or review?*
- *Thanks for letting me know. Is your budget renewed annually or quarterly?*
- *Does not having a budget mean we will never get a chance to do business together this year?*

Objection: "I Need a Discount"
Honest Negotiation Responses

- *Discount?*
- *It's good of you to be looking for the best deal. How much of a discount do you need? Why that much?*
- *Making sure you're getting the best deal for your company is a good idea. If we can't budge on the price, does that mean it's over between us?*

Echo! Echo!
Another option for asking questions is to use the echo technique. The echo technique is simply the art of taking the last

word (or last important word) in a client's sentence and turning it into a question.

One of our clients uses the echo technique every time one of her clients objects to her price. Our client's company sells multimillion dollar custom software development services to companies in the resources industry, so as you can imagine, they tend to face a lot of pricing objections.

Whenever a client says, *"I need a discount,"* their sales reps look them squarely in the eye and say, *"discount?"* Ninety-nine times out of a hundred, the client either tells the rep exactly what needs to be done from a price and terms point of view to move the deal forward or offers alternatives to the pricing model that will make both parties happy.

What could be simpler than that?

The Start of a Brilliant Career

On a personal note, it was silence combined with a question that won Colleen her first-ever professional negotiation.

She was 22, fresh out of college, in her first sales job and had never negotiated anything on her own. Colleen was working with one of her company's clients on a large employee benefits program and everything was approved when the client turned to her and said:

"Hey, Colleen, everything looks good. I just need a 10 percent discount."

Colleen had no idea what to do so was quiet for a few seconds and then said something terribly eloquent and persuasive, like "huh?" The client responded by saying he "just had to ask," and they did the deal without the discount.

What's the moral of the story? Don't be afraid of objections and negotiating. If you follow this simple two-step formula—

be silent and ask questions—you'll find that you can handle almost any objection easily, honestly, and profitably.

Summing Up

When was the last time that you felt someone was really listening to you? How did it make you feel? Pretty good, right? Our job in sales is to make the client feel good. One way to ensure that is to listen—really listen—with the intent to understand. We have to read between the lines for the real message when working with clients. Often what the client says and what the client means are two different things. Have you had this experience? When someone complains, do you hear just the complaints, or do you take the time to recognize the message behind the complaints? When the client wants to negotiate, do you stop and take the time to find out what they really want in the contract?

Remember, the client has every right to raise objections or make comments. The worst thing we can do is to try to justify our position or defend our prices. As lawyers have known for centuries, nothing makes an innocent person look guiltier than trying too hard to protest his innocence.

Selling is about helping your prospects solve a problem, not about trying to force them to see your point of view. Objections mean your prospect is asking for help, and you are in a position to help. Be prepared, ask questions, listen, don't panic, and engage.

Turning a Onetime Client into a Lifetime Client

By now you know our passion for honest communication and you know why we're such advocates for it. That's right. Honest communication is the most important sales strategy for long-term business growth. Since this is a book about sales, we have primarily focused on making sales and gaining new clients. An essential component of the sales process is retaining clients and growing with them. This is the key to real success in sales and the key to organizational success, as well.

Before we look at some best practices for managing ongoing client relationships, let's look briefly at some of the trouble that commonly arises in those relationships:

- Your client purchases a product or service, and it doesn't meet expectations.
- Your client does not receive the product or service within the promised timeframe.
- Your client is happy with the purchase, but the ongoing service does not provide what the client needs.
- Your client is pleased with the product or service but is disappointed with the post-sale follow-up.

While some of these issues may sound dire, all of them can be dealt with. The key is to have a sound plan for handling post-sale client relationships, and that plan should be founded on (you guessed it!) honest communication.

Increase Your Profits by over 75 Percent

According to Fred Reichheld, author of *The Loyalty Effect: The Hidden Force Behind Growth, Profits and Lasting Value*, U.S. companies lose half of their clients every five years, and those losses hit businesses right in their bottom lines. The great news is that we also know that a 5 percent increase in client retention can increase your profits by between 75 and 95 percent.

The percentage increase will vary by industry type and this large increase in profits is the result of three major factors:

- Increased client retention means bigger revenues because every time you lose a client it takes time and money to find a replacement. Our own studies have shown that selling to new clients takes 80 percent longer than selling more to existing clients.

- Selling more to existing clients is 5 to 15 times *less expensive* than acquiring a new client (due to less advertising and direct mail as well as time savings).

- Loyal clients referring you to their families, friends, and colleagues, further reduces the cost of acquiring new clients and the time it takes to close new business.

These factors make it obvious that client retention and referrals are worth their weight in gold. For that reason, we would like to share some of the best practices of firms that excel in client retention and increasing the bottom line. The key to making all of these best practices work is to implement the honest communication strategies learned in this book.

Best Practice One: Know Your Clients

To serve a good client well (and to decide which clients deserve the best service), you have to understand how they operate, who makes their decisions, and their strategic direction. Salespeople can collect this information by writing up account plans for the largest or most profitable accounts (those in the top 30 percent).

These plans should include the following information:

- A review of the client's industry.
- The client's revenue projections.
- Your position in the industry.
- The threats to your position.
- Plans to expand within the account.
- Your most recent client-satisfaction results.
- A plan for building and maintaining executive relationships.

Salespeople should review these detailed account plans with executives to get additional insights on how to maximize the opportunities presented. These account plans are an excellent tool for maintaining service and sales relationships even as an organization experiences staff turnover.

Of course, anybody can write up these plans, but if the input isn't accurate they won't be effective. Remember our discussion of facts versus assumptions. Work with your clients to get the unsaid said and maintain an open dialogue. If you do that, your account plans will serve you and your company well.

Best Practice Two: Follow Up

Have you ever lost contact with a client and wondered why?

Maybe a client stopped reordering from you for no apparent reason. Or perhaps they stopped calling you or even returning your calls, and for the life of you, you can't figure out what went wrong.

The answer could be entirely out of your hands. The client might have changed jobs and forgotten to let you know. The client's son or daughter may have started working for your closest competitor. Or perhaps the client inherited a fortune from a long-lost uncle and decided to take up immediate residence on a private island in the South Pacific.

Or it could be that maybe you yourself broke the "contact chain," and allowed the client to drift away for good.

The Contact Chain

Staying in contact with clients is an essential part of sales success.

For most of us, it's easy to remember to communicate with our families, coworkers, and friends. After all, we tend to see or chat with them on a weekly or daily basis.

Your clients, on the other hand, aren't likely to be hanging out at the neighborhood pub or waiting with dinner when you come home each night. Your clients may not even be in the same time zone as you, let alone the same zip or area code. Because clients aren't an automatic part of our daily lives, it can be all too easy to take them for granted or let them slip our minds.

In our work as coaches, we have seen far too many of our clients lose contact with their clients because they assumed the clients would get in touch with them whenever they needed something. By not proactively maintaining their existing contacts and following up on leads, they run the risk of losing a lot of deals—and a lot of business.

Client Contact Tips

How can you stay in touch with your clients on a regular basis? Start by remembering some basic rules of etiquette. Then try incorporating the following seven habits into your sales regimen:

1. When addressing an e-mail or letter, always begin with the person's name—even if finding or remembering it is a nuisance. People respond best when they read or hear their name being used. Always say "Dear Name," "Hi Name," or "Hello Name" when addressing a client. Using "hey" or, even worse, no salutation at all simply does not cut it.

2. Plan regular contacts with all your clients. According to the American Marketing Association, people can handle up to 200 contacts per year. Even we think that might be a little overkill, so how about agreeing to contact your clients once every two weeks? This will help guarantee that your clients never get the chance to forget who you are or slip away unnoticed.

3. If clients contact you first, thank them for getting in touch. In your next e-mail or on the phone, start the conversation with something like: "Thank you for your note, it's great to hear from you."

4. Never multitask when talking to a client. I can't stress this enough. In the era of BlackBerrys, cell phones, and Bluetooth, we all think we can do a thousand things at

once. If you're checking your e-mail or updating your schedule while on the phone with a client, believe me— they can tell! Whether you're with your client in person or on the phone, give the other person your full attention. Turn off the cell phone, e-mail, or PDA and stay focused on the person you're actually talking to. This won't result in you missing out on other opportunities. It will increase your likelihood of getting more business from the client you're with.

5. Show your sincere appreciation. Every time a client buys something from you, gives you a referral, or goes out of his way for you, don't just sit back and expect that he will continue to do so in the future. Acknowledge what he has done and thank him for his business, assistance, or generosity. Remember: reciprocity is, by definition, a two-way street. When people give you something and you don't acknowledge it, most of them will think long and hard before helping you again.

6. If you haven't heard from a client because they are out of the office, busy, sick, traveling, or just plain ignoring you, don't stop trying to reach them. Keeping the lines of communication open will maximize the chances that you will get a response when the person is better positioned to give you one. If your usual methods of communicating aren't working, try something innovative, like sending a message by courier, fax, or snail mail. Sometimes simply shaking up the way you communicate is enough to recapture a client's attention.

7. Last and most definitely not least, always think of your clients first and put their needs ahead of your own. This doesn't have to be a grand gesture or heroic act of self-

sacrifice. The next time you read an article that you think might interest your client, just send it along with a little note (if appropriate) that says: "I thought this might be of interest to you."

If you're guilty of not following some of the tips outlined above, you could be about to lose more clients faster than you realized. If that's the case, now is the time to get out there and start renewing those relationships. Because in the end, it's always more profitable to sell more to your existing clients than it is to have to find new ones.

Best Practice Three: Don't Oversell and Underdeliver

This is probably the most important best practice in client retention. We're sure you have seen how deals go sour when an overexuberant salesperson on the brink of closing the deal has said: *"Mr. Buyer, this product is exciting because not only will it give you what you wanted (which you need), but also these other features (which you didn't ask for)."* In that situation the client might be tempted to ask whether they should be paying for extra features they don't require. Furthermore, the expectations may have just gone through the roof. Be careful. Be honest. Let's look at some specific tips for avoiding the overselling trap.

Confirm the Client's Criteria for Success

The first step in avoiding overselling and underdelivering is to determine what is most important to the parties involved. Be sure that your definition of success is consistent with everyone else's definition. Remember, people often operate from their assumptions and what *they* think is important rather than finding out what is actually important to the client.

Ask questions such as:

- *"You mentioned that A, B, and C are important to you. Which is the most important?"*
- *"When you say you don't want to spend too much, what exactly do you mean?"*
- *"What are your most important criteria for success?"*

The technique of asking leading, open-ended questions is a great help when potential clients are being vague. Sometimes people are vague because they don't want to speak the truth and be held accountable. Sometimes people are vague because they really don't know the answer or haven't thought through it. Great salespeople and great client service representatives excel at helping the client come to clarity. Why? Because we cannot successfully sell or deliver good service if we are not clear about a client's needs and wants.

Here's a situation that benefited from going back to the client and confirming the criteria for success:

Bob and his associates were experiencing some high-stress miscommunications with their own client and they wanted some help. The root of the problem turned out to be a lack of clarity in what their client wanted. Bob was reluctant to pursue greater clarity because his company was already trying to execute the deliverables. Pretty tough to do when you're not sure what you're delivering! Of course things were stressful. Although Bob's client had committed to the contract, the lack of clarity was on its way toward breaking the deal. Trying to deliver on something without full understanding is a real waste of time and resources. After they learned some specific strategies for engaging in upfront, honest conversations,

Bob and his associates were able to gain the clarity they needed and execute the contract. In the end, everyone was satisfied and the work was quite profitable for Bob's company.

If people are vague, we must help them be clear. We gain clarity by asking probing questions. People can sometimes get upset about being asked a lot of questions, so make sure you show empathy when asking the questions and explain that your questions are intended to help you better serve their needs, prevent misunderstandings, and deliver what they are looking for.

Here is a list of questions that may be helpful to you in the quest for clarity:

- What are your top three priorities for defining the success of this project?
- Specifically, what is most important to you?
- When you reflect on this project, what needs to be in place for you to feel that it has been a complete success?
- What does success on this project look like to you?
- Is this something you would expect us to do or do you expect to handle it?
- Can you give me some more background on that?
- Can you give me an example?
- When you say _____ (insert vague word here), what do you mean by that?
- Is that something that is critical?
- How important is that compared with_____ (insert some other criterion as a point of comparison)?

If the person still has trouble being specific, make some suggestions to help them. Think of an eye doctor trying to find the right lens. The doctor keeps flipping different lenses in front of your eye, asking: "Is this better? Or this?"

You might start the conversation like this:

"John, when I speak to executives like yourself, most often they tell me that although their business is going great, they have concerns about_____ (name a problem your product addresses). Is that an example of what you were talking about earlier (reference the point you are trying to get clarity around)?"

The key is to pick a few serious or common problems that your product can solve. This way, you are almost guaranteed your client will say: *"Yes, that's a problem for me, too!"* Follow up by asking your prospect to be more specific about the problems they are facing. Sometimes it's easier for people to discuss the issues they're having when they know that others are facing them, too. Remember that as a general rule, a salesperson and others who are interacting with the client should do the talking 20 to 30 percent of the time; the remaining 70 to 80 percent of the time, the prospect should be talking.

These conversations will enable you to determine the criteria for success—and that is information you need to have. Inevitably, whether your client states the criteria for success or not, you will be judged by that standard. Better to know it, and to know it early. That understanding will create a win-win situation for you and your client and ultimately lead to ongoing sales and service as well as referrals. Again, honest communication is the only way to uncover the real criteria for success.

Best Practice Four: At the Same Time Don't Underpromise and Overdeliver

When you underpromise and overdeliver, you set the bar for what the client expects you to deliver at a whole new level. What you overdelivered becomes the new baseline, and when you aren't able to meet this new standard consistently, your client will end up feeling confused, disappointed—or betrayed.

For instance, say you get a client to place an order by promising a large price discount if they buy before the end of the month. You've made a sale, but what happens next quarter or next month when they need to reorder? They'll expect that same discount again, and if you can't give it to them, they'll simply wait until the end of the month, when you'll be feeling the pressure to sell and will be more likely to cave on the price.

The key is to be honest and empathetic toward the perspective of your client. This doesn't guarantee that the client will be happy. But it beats the alternative—failing to meet someone's expectations, having trust erode, and losing future sales. This isn't always fair. We understand sometimes you want to go the extra mile for your customer and you should. Just remember that to build a consistently profitable relationship, there's no point in delivering better, faster, or cheaper than your original promise if you know that you can't do it that way again the next time. It's better to simply say what you are going to do, and then do it exactly as and when you said you would.

Best Practice Five: Clean Up Mistakes along the Way

Managing client relationships also requires addressing mistakes in a timely manner. If you have had a track record of not keeping your promises with a client, come clean.

First, admit to the client that you have not always kept your promises. Seriously. If your clients have been on the receiving end of your late or incomplete work in the past, your candor will be the first (and best) step to rebuilding your relationship with them. And, after you come clean, you must commit to keeping your word in the future. If for some reason you are unable to keep a promise, you must let your client know as soon as you know.

Second, provide specifics about what will be done differently to rectify the situation so that it will not happen again. Let's face it. We have all had the experience of people apologizing when they make mistakes, but then they keep on making the same mistakes. Needless to say, that is no way to maintain client relationships. Once you acknowledge what has gone wrong, you must outline exactly what is going to be different and then make sure to make it happen.

Best Practice Six: Say No and Keep the Deal Alive

Managing expectations plays an important role in being sure not to oversell and underdeliver. As you know, there is a heavy price to pay when expectations aren't managed properly. Trust is broken and sales are missed despite much hard work.

Once you have completed a full analysis of a prospect's situation and understand what the client wants, be upfront about whether you can meet those expectations. Remember, it's useless (and damaging) to withhold the truth and promise something that can't be delivered on time.

Setting the right expectations sometimes means having to say no. Most salespeople are afraid to say no. Why? They mistakenly fear that they will lose a sale if they don't always say yes.

In fact, no fear could be more unfounded. In sales, saying no doesn't have to be a relationship-ender. Instead, you just need to find a way to say no so that your client realizes how he will benefit from your truthful answers.

Try some of the following techniques for saying no while still keeping the sale alive:

- "I am not able to make it Tuesday at 2:00 P.M. Are you able to meet at 10:00 A.M. instead?"
- "I would love to tell you that the product will be delivered by Friday. There is a good chance that it won't. Could we agree on a Tuesday deadline?"

These statements do not guarantee that the client will be happy. Nothing does! They do offer benefits to the client as well as to you. Plus, they are far better than the alternative: failing to deliver what you promised, falling short of your client's expectations, or submitting shoddy work on time.

Remember: anything other than the truth erodes trust and makes your word worthless.

In the Process of Managing Client Expectations, Remember These Three Keys

1. Be direct and clear about what you can and cannot get done.
2. Emphasize the benefit to your client.
3. Offer a suggestion that addresses your client's needs.

If your client's expectations are unreasonable or impossible, you owe it to yourself, your company, and the client to say so. While this may initially rock the boat, clients who are serious about doing business with you—and who want to build a long-term, profitable relationship—will sincerely appreciate your honesty and will likely be even more willing to work with you to establish more reasonable expectations.

For instance, you could say something like this:

"Yes, we could deliver this additional service/product as you requested. I am concerned, though, that given the allocated resources, the overall quality could suffer. Because this is beyond the scope of our current agreement, we would need to eliminate something else or increase the fee. Another option would be to add one month to our deadline. Since you mentioned you had some flexibility, this would allow us to reallocate our resources accordingly. If we do that, we could add in what you want without having to increase your investment. Is that agreeable?"

As you can see, this dialogue corresponds to the three steps we just mentioned.

Shared expectations produce greater harmony and more sales—period. When establishing expectations at the outset of a project, be as thorough as possible, and be prepared to adjust as needed.

For example, if you find the client asking for something you simply can't deliver, try one of the following to set the right expectations from the start:

- "I'm not sure we can provide the product you are looking for at that price. If not, does that mean we will not move forward?"
- "That color has been out of stock for weeks and I know that I can't get it for you on this order. Does that mean we can't go ahead?"
- "I don't think we can meet your delivery schedule. Knowing that, does it make sense for us to move forward?"

Sure, some of these examples seem direct. The reason that they work is because they get to the real reason your client might be objecting or asking for the impossible. Besides, if your client is asking for something that you can't deliver, and it's critical to their decision, isn't it better to know that up front?

In addition, be clear about what your client can expect from you, as well as what they can't. Tell the client what you can deliver, even if it is not necessarily what they are asking for. Tell the client that if ever you are unable to fulfill a request, you will always let them know the minute you realize it yourself.

Best Practice Seven: Interview Your Clients

To maintain profitable, long-term relationships, the best salespeople make a habit of checking up on all their existing business relationships on a regular basis to ensure that they are continuing to achieve their—and their clients'— goals.

We suggest to our clients that they carry out these in-depth interviews about once every three months depending on how often they are in touch with their clients for other reasons (such as regular sales or service items). Following up with clients is important at all times. It is even more so when you sense that there may be a problem brewing, such as when you feel someone isn't listening, when you aren't getting any real feedback, or when you feel you simply aren't getting along with the other person.

Letting things go in the hope that "time will heal all things" is never a wise course of action. If time healed all wounds, we wouldn't need divorce lawyers, therapists—or to serve alcohol at high school reunions. If anything, time can make some wounds smart even more. So if you feel you may have a problem in the making with one of your clients, solve it now, before it gets beyond your ability to mend.

If you don't know how often to check in with your clients ask them! An effective trust-building question is: *"I want to ensure that I provide you with the best service possible. What does that look like to you?"*

The following three-step process can help you check up on your relationships with your clients, to make sure they stay as strong tomorrow as they are today. One more thing to remember: Never conduct a client checkup by e-mail. While technology is wonderful, it lacks the personal touch of a phone call or, ideally, a face-to-face meeting, which you'll sorely need if there is any mending to do.

Step 1. *Get Curious.* First, start your checkup by asking any or all of the following questions:

- I want to ensure that I offer you the best service possible. What does that look like to you?

- On a scale of 1 to10, how well are we doing? What would it take to be a 10?

- Do you feel that I listen to you—really listen, hear, and understand you? If you really don't listen to the other person, admit it, and ask what could be done to improve things.

Note: Never respond to a client's feedback with *"Yes, but . . ."* or *"I know."* These phrases will discourage your client from responding openly and honestly. It's extremely hard for people to give honest feedback, so no matter what they say, don't debate them, make excuses, or try to justify why you acted the way you did. Just thank them for their candor, then after the meeting is over, consider what they had to say carefully and with as little ego as possible.

Try on their feedback like a shirt. If it fits, use it. If not, discard it. But before you discard anything, remember the old saying: "If three people call you a horse, you'd better start looking for a saddle." If you feel hurt or defensive, there is likely some truth to the comment. If it weren't true, it wouldn't be so upsetting.

Step 2. *Document Action Steps.* While you're still on the phone or in the meeting with your client, immediately commit to an action that you can unilaterally take to improve the relationship based on the feedback the client has given you. This will encourage your client to take action as well, and things will almost certainly improve.

For example, if your client feels you don't give them enough advance notice before dropping by, tell the client that from now on, you will always e-mail ahead to schedule a meeting rather than simply calling or stopping in unannounced and interrupting their day. Then, make sure to do it, without fail.

Step 3. *Check In.* Lastly, arrange a follow-up meeting to check how things are going as a result of the changes you've made in your relationship.

Gain mutual agreement about when the next meeting will be, to ensure you don't cross the line between persistence and stalking. Choose an appropriate method of following up, such as a phone call or an invitation to lunch, dinner, or coffee. Another effective approach is to send a brief e-mail to your client summarizing the meeting or phone call and documenting the actions you have both committed to taking.

When following up, go back to Step 1, and repeat these steps as needed.

In our experience, the insights you can gain by conducting this simple checkup can be profound, and profoundly rewarding. Your job during this interview—as with all sales conversations is to ensure clients feel better after the interaction with you than they did before. Listening to them, really listening, with the intent of understanding them, is one of the best ways we know to make that goal a reality.

Another Way to Gain This Information Is Through a Third-Party Interview

A best practice many financial advisors use is the third-party interview. We think this concept can be used by any company in any market. The idea is that sometimes clients may be more honest with a neutral interviewer than they will be with you. That may be true. An effective client management strategy would be to follow our three-step check-in process with a client on a periodic basis and also use a third-party interview to validate your findings. That way you can be sure to gather the most detailed and accurate information from the client.

The third-party interview is an effective technique because clients often do not say the things that you need to hear the most directly to you. However, they aren't so reticent—or flattering—when a third party asks them for feedback. Consider hiring one of the many consulting companies or telemarketing firms to conduct client-satisfaction surveys on your behalf. It could make all the difference in future sales and client relationships.

Be sure to double-check all information you gather. Remember, just because a client says they are happy, may not mean they are really happy. If you assume at face value without asking any further questions, you may be disappointed later.

Summing Up

It's much easier—and more profitable—to keep an existing customer than it is to land a new one.

Don't believe us? Just look at the numbers.

Research tells us that most U.S. companies lose half of their clients every five years. We also know that as little as a

5 percent increase in client retention can increase profits by a whopping 75 to 95 percent. While this percentage can vary by industry, the overwhelming increase in profits is caused by three major factors:

1. Lower costs—selling to existing clients is between 5 and 15 times less expensive (and takes far less of your time) than acquiring a new customer.
2. More referrals—satisfied clients are only too happy to refer you to their friends and colleagues, further reducing the time and cost of landing new business.
3. Greater revenues—every time you lose a loyal client, you also lose the revenue stream they generated until you can find a new client to take the old one's place.

The key to keeping your clients happy is to find out precisely what motivates them, what is most important to them, and what they want most. Then, simply find the product that gives them what they want at the best value.

Who are your customers, and what do they really want?

Knowing the answer—not assuming the answer—will ensure that you build long-lasting profitable relationships in sales.

Remember to Practice Honesty Internally

A company can only be as good with the client as the company is internally. Yes, salespeople can make the sale, but if the company doesn't deliver according to expectations, then the possibility of losing that client is very real. And let's not forget the Internet. Losing one client is bad enough, but having millions hear about it is even worse.

We are only as strong externally as we are internally. If your company is disorganized or internal departments are not coordinating with each other to serve your clients effectively, things will begin to unravel. Ongoing sales and service are impossible without internal honesty. History shows us that people eventually find out the truth, so it's best to be up-front.

Stick to these four nonnegotiable strategies for internal honesty and you won't go wrong.

Keep Commitments

Hold everyone accountable to their commitments and follow up with your internal partners to ensure timelines and deliverables will be met as expected. If you tolerate commitments slipping past their due dates, clients will become frustrated and leave. As a sales professional, the buck stops with you. You are responsible for following up internally to ensure client projects are on time, and you are responsible for communicating regularly to the client. Take ownership.

Okay. Realistically, sometimes commitments do slip. If this happens ensure the new commitment is communicated quickly to everyone—internal and external (the client) so that plans can be adjusted and expectations managed by the sales team. While you can't be responsible for everyone's work ethic internally, you can be responsible for communicating the plan or revised plan to the client in a timely and honest way.

Focus on Interdepartmental Honest Communication and Teamwork

Helping each other and working together within your organization creates goodwill internally and externally. For example, salespeople should help the technical experts with implementation guidelines, and the technical experts should assist the salespeople by looking for new opportunities while on-site. Besides the ongoing feelings of goodwill, this will dramatically increase the bottom line. The discussion of ideas and opportunities across department lines is like cross-pollination. Everyone benefits.

As a quick side note: Are your company's nonsalespeople trained to see opportunities and pass them along? If not, you are losing out on thousands of dollars of potential revenue each year. Train everyone who interacts with the client to see and pass along opportunities. Everybody sells.

Even if your organization isn't training everyone to spot opportunities you can make networking a priority for yourself. Here are some benefits to you as a salesperson networking within your own company and with other sales reps:

- The opportunity to hear about company capabilities that you're not fully familiar with and for others to hear about what you're doing.

- The opportunity to pass on leads and ideas to others and create reciprocity (in other words, to have them do the same for you).

- The opportunity to hear valuable lessons learned from business that has been won and lost.
- The opportunity to develop closer ties with client service professionals and hear their ideas.

We were once touring a top rated inbound client service call center and noticed a designated "listening room" where employees could don a headset and listen to the conversations without being heard. In fact, it was a requirement for each executive to spend a set number of hours in the listening room each quarter.

While a listening room is not an uncommon practice for a call center, the intent of this listening room was unique because its purpose was not for executives to listen and judge the call center workers. Rather the listening room was designed to capture the comments, suggestions, and ideas from the clients who were calling.

These call center executives knew that the best way to understand what clients wanted was to listen to them directly.

- The opportunity to network with other employees who interact with the clients. For instance, your professional services or implementation teams who have regular client interaction might hear of opportunities and ideas for sole source and new services.

Appreciate Each Other

Not only do people often withhold information and opportunities from each other, but people often withhold their compliments and appreciation for others. This negatively affects honest communication. When people don't feel appreciated, they are less open with the expression of their thoughts and ideas.

How often do people within your organization express appreciation to each other and to clients? This sounds like a no-brainer. Sadly, people don't appreciate others frequently enough when the truth is you can never appreciate others too frequently. People want to be appreciated for their contributions and acknowledged for their efforts. We have never heard of an employee or client leaving because they received too much appreciation. Have you?

We have certainly heard of people leaving because they received too little appreciation. What are you and your company doing to express appreciation to your clients? If the answer is "not much," you might want to examine whether this is damaging your referrals and your client retention rate.

While you're at it, if an internal partner (administration, finance, shipping, installation, and so on) provides you exceptional service in helping secure or keep a client, why not thank them formally? A card is a great idea; a coffee is nice, too!

Partner and Vendor Honesty

In today's complex business world, we need others to help execute and deliver the product or service we're selling. For example, in the defense industry one company might be a subcontractor to another, and then in another situation the contractor and subcontractor roles might be reversed. In other situations, we create a network of vendors to coordinate while we are the interface with the client.

You cannot maintain ongoing client relationships without partner and vendor honesty. If everyone on the project doesn't abide by the principles of honest communication and doesn't see value in properly managing expectations, you will find yourself in situations where partners have overpromised. You might suddenly be expected to hold to a deadline you never agreed to. You might suddenly be expected to pay a fee that was not agreed to, or you may be forced to deliver a product with features that were not approved. Unfortunately, in a situation like this we know that it's always you, the sales rep, who will get blamed.

If you are working with a vendor or partner who does not subscribe to honest principles, you could be walking into a time bomb . . . with no idea when it could go off! You may never get what you want, need, or expect. Here's a good example of a bad situation.

Amanda and her company were working on a full-service solution for their client and they were coordinating with several vendors. One piece of the package was some software. Amanda suggested a particular piece of software and the client agreed. But the software vendor never told Amanda that it was planning to eventually discontinue the software. The software was implemented as part of Amanda's solution for her client's situation, and when the vendor suddenly shared that it was going to discontinue the software and eventually its support of the software, Amanda was left in an awful situation.

This situation makes it easy to see the value of doing business with honest, reliable vendors. We advise you to use the same honest communication principles discussed in *Honesty Sells* with your clients as well as with your vendors and partners. Make sure your vendors share your philosophy that honesty sells. If not, do not do business with them. If you do, you risk your reputation and future sales. By all means, remember the Internet and the impact a disgruntled client can make.

Summing Up

Honest communication is the most important sales strategy for long-term business growth, because it is a strategy that addresses sales as well as ongoing client service and retention.

The four steps in this chapter are proven strategies for meeting client needs and maintaining healthy, positive relationships with clients, which translate into more sales and more profit.

When it comes to managing postsale client relationships, the internal dynamics of an organization truly matter. Salespeople may make the sale but every part of the organization is responsible for keeping the client satisfied. Probing and honest communication is the way to get to the bottom of things and provide the service that every client wants and deserves. Internal honesty plays a crucial role in selling more, increasing client retention, and gaining referrals—all of which will make a major impact on your company's bottom line.

There are many additional strategies, techniques, and tools that can be implemented in the quest for internal honesty; we've only discussed four. And, there are entire books written on the subject, including Steven Gaffney's *Just Be Honest* and *Honesty Works*. You can also visit the *Honesty Sells* web site at www.honestysells.com for ideas and updates on best practices for implementing honesty in your selling environment now.

Some Final Thoughts

No legacy is so rich as honesty.

—William Shakespeare

Honesty sells is the best long-term sales success strategy.

Honest selling builds trust between you and your client base. Trust is the foundation of all relationships. As you become skilled in distinguishing what you notice from what you imagine, you can help other people accomplish the same thing (remember the Law of Reciprocity). This can be a real gift for the people you sell to who are not always giving you the information you need in order to help them want to buy from you.

Do You Need to Use Everything That We Have Offered in This Book?

No.

In fact, if you try to use everything, likely you will wind up not using any of it. Review the scenarios that resonated with you, study the techniques offered, and put them into practice. It all starts with one step. Begin by making one small change in the way you relate to others.

Finally, we would like to leave you with these six points:

1. Honesty sells! Honesty is the strategy for long-term sales success and profitability. Sure you can close a sale today and make a quick buck with a lie. But you can only sustain that relationship for a lifetime with honest selling practices.
2. Do not make assumptions.

3. Build an honest sales zone by soliciting and providing referrals. Referrals close 15 times faster and are more profitable than any other lead you can generate. The best way to receive more referrals from clients, partners, and friends is to practice honest selling principles.

4. Practice honest principles with all internal and external relationships for the best and most profitable sales.

5. It's not how smooth you are, it's how honest you are that matters. If you stumble in your words, your sincerity will be compelling and endearing such that you'll win business and keep clients for life.

6. The most profitable sales are those made through your existing client relationships. If your clients like you and trust you, they will be honest with you. Only then can you increase your sales by selling more to existing customers.

As we indicated in the introductory chapter of this book, the advice we're offering is not always easy to follow. Much of it involves unlearning old habits and adopting a new approach to doing business with people. It requires a commitment to learn, to self-examine, and to change.

The payoff can be lucrative!

Building an open, honest, and profitable relationship with your clients is more than a sales gimmick—it's a time-tested and field-tested approach that works. The proof is in the success—year after year—enjoyed by the top 10 percent of sales performers in every organization. You can achieve the same results that they do.

Honest, open communications is a journey—and one that really has no end—but it starts with a commitment. The rewards become apparent through perseverance.

The results are clear and hard to dispute: You'll sell more in less time.

ABOUT THE AUTHORS

Steven Gaffney

For the past 15 years, Steven Gaffney has been a leading expert on honest interpersonal communication, influence, and leadership. Today Steven is one of the most recognized authorities on the subject of honesty.

Given Steven's inability to speak due to hearing impairments as a child, he learned at a very early age the importance of communication. This problem stimulated Steven's desire to help individuals transform the quality of their lives through honest and effective communication, and is the foundation of the Steven Gaffney Company.

Steven developed The Honest Communication Results System™, a simple and effective method of communicating that has empowered individuals to speak to anyone, about anything, at any time. This system is highlighted in his two best-selling books *Just Be Honest: Authentic Communication Strategies That Get Results and Last a Lifetime* and *Honesty Works! Real-World Solutions to Common Problems at Work and Home*.

He has also developed proven communication systems, including The Honest Presentations Systems™, The Honest Achievement Results System™, and The Honest Leadership Results System™.

Steven's services have been sought out by a diverse range of leaders and top executives of multinational corporations such as Marriott, Lockheed Martin, Raytheon, BP, Citigroup, Allstate Insurance, Blue Cross Blue Shield of Michigan, Best Buy, NASA, American Cancer Society, the U.S. Navy, SAIC, American Express, Blue Care Network of Michigan, the Oncology Nursing Association, and many others. He also works with top leaders in the military, speakers, writers, entertainers, teachers, parents, and couples.

Steven Gaffney has been interviewed or featured in major media and publications including CBS, NBC, FOX, the *Wall Street Journal,* the *Washington Post, Entrepreneur* magazine, and *USA Today*, as well as numerous national and local radio programs in cities across the country. Steven also produced and hosted his own cable access show, *Maximum Effectiveness*, where he interviewed successful individuals to reveal the secrets of their success.

Steven serves as a relationship expert for BettyConfidential.com, a growing online community for women. His column shares tips and advice to guide women from all walks of life in their quest for happier, healthier relationships in their work and home life. He has also partnered with Professionals in the City, a social networking organization, to conduct seminars specifically for women.

Earlier in his career, Gaffney founded two non-profit organizations including POWER—People Organized for World Empowerment and Results, a non-profit organization that provides speakers and trainers to charitable organizations.

Steven is a member of the National Speakers Association, and his programs consistently receive high ratings, with attendees and participants reporting immediate, sustainable results. He is also a former adjunct faculty member of The Johns Hopkins University, as well as former board member of the Washington, D.C. chapter of Sales and Marketing Executives International. Thousands of people across the nation credit Steven's speaking engagements, seminars, television and radio appearances, books and multimedia products with making immediate and lasting positive changes in both their organizations as well as their personal lives.

Steven was born in Stockholm, Sweden, to American parents. He is a graduate of James Madison University and now resides in Arlington, Virginia.

Colleen Francis

Colleen is driven by a passion for sales—and results. A successful sales professional for over 15 years, she understands the challenges of selling in today's market and how traditional sales techniques from decades ago often fall short.

Colleen has studied the habits of the top 10 percent of sales performers from organizations of all sizes and shapes—from Fortune 500 companies to small businesses. She has complemented conventional wisdom of the sales process with these proven techniques for *a sales approach that gets results today.*

Through her company, Engage Selling Solutions, Colleen has condensed this winning formula into an internationally acclaimed sales training system, helping sales professionals everywhere get results. Through key note speaking, sales training and sales coaching, Colleen delivers her savvy, no-nonsense approach to sales, rooted in the belief that there really isn't a single magic formula to success. Rather, her researched, field-tested approach is about consistently applying a common sense process for listening to, working with, and tending to the needs of customers.

Ask any of Colleen's clients about why they call on her services—again and again—and you'll hear a common refrain:

she delivers results! Her refreshing candor, her genuine, sincere message, and the personal experiences she relates as a top-ranked sales executive all are inspiring motivators for sales professionals who strive to get to the top . . . and stay there. Just as important, Colleen is unwavering in her commitment to sales training that makes a lasting and meaningful impact on the corporate bottom line. That's why her services are regularly sought by leading private and public sector organizations across North America like RBC, Adecco, Bell, Dow Chemical, HelmsBrisco, Corel, and many others.

Colleen has been distinguished by the Canadian Professional Sales Association as a Certified Sales Professional (C.S.P.) and is 2008 President of the Canadian Association of Professional Speakers. *Sales and Marketing* magazine has called Colleen and Engage Selling *one of the top five most effective sales-training organizations in the market today!*

INDEX